Living Under the Sovereign Hand of God

The Story of Ruth

Real People, Real Issues, Real Answers

Michael McCutcheon

About the Front Cover.....

Photo by: Ari Sheridan, ari@teamsheridan.com

Naomi by Retha Storey Heintz, Ruth by Amy Schubert, Orpah by Loren Keller

Sifted Publications
Luke 22:31-32
Joliet, IL   60433-9567
USA

www.xulonpress.com

Thank you for all your help . . .

There are five people I both need and want to thank for all their help in making this book what it has become.

Craig and Janet Larabee were members of the very first church I pastored in Lincoln, NE. They allowed me to sit at their dining room table uninterrupted for hours on end for a whole week and pound out the original manuscript on my laptop. Thank you Craig and Janet!

Charles and Aretha Heintz are my friends; they love the Lord Jesus and each other for many, many years. Together they possess a great deal of spiritual wisdom. Each morning they read through the original manuscript together during their devotions and also gave several suggestions which were added into the revised manuscript. Thank you Charles and Aretha!

Then over a period of seven months I met for 2 to 3 hours per week with Kelly Corcoran, a former missionary to Guatemala. Kelly brutally challenged every word, every thought, every concept, every Scripture passage — she challenged everything but the page numbers. Each week she attacked a few more pages and held me answerable for everything I had written and for things I had left unwritten. She even questioned my male line of thinking as I wrote a book about which the two main participants were women. But in the end, the manuscript became a much more clear and concise message. Thank you, Kelly!

Without the help of these friends, this book would not be the book I hope you are about to read.

Throughout this study on the Story of Ruth, there are three graphics; each one giving different messages.

Periodically throughout this book about Ruth, this graphic appears with some questions to think about in regard to the teaching that was just presented. It is meant to stimulate our thinking just a little bit more.

At other times there will be this graphic which will represent our need to keep "digging deeper" into a topic in the text, or it will introduce new information, or give some new background information relevant to the ideas just presented.

 At the end of each chapter, this graphic appears with some concluding remarks or questions to discuss as we "wrap up" the scene.

As you can see, this study is meant to be interactive and the three graphics above draw us by various means into the substance of the text.

Graphics developed by Dan Laib Studios, Joliet, IL. www.danlaibstudios.com

Preface to the Story of Ruth

The book of Ruth is often misunderstood and prejudged. Sometimes people will consider it to be mainly a women's study. Several think it is only a love story and fail to understand its true significance. Others feel it has no relation to their lives today. Yet after each time I would finish leading a study on the book of Ruth, I would remind the people of their initial responses and asked them if they still thought the same way. Most agreed that this study had opened their minds and hearts to a whole new dimension regarding the person of Ruth and the book that bears her name.

We often tend to think we today have new issues that have never been felt by Believers in the past, but that is not true. First Corinthians 10:13 (NLT) tells us, **The temptations in your life are no different from what others experience.** *And God is faithful. He will not allow the temptation to be more than you can stand. When you are tempted, he will show you a way out so that you can endure* (emphasis mine).And again in King Solomon's book of Ecclesiastes, *What has been will be again, what has been done will be done again; there is nothing new under the sun. Is there anything of which one can say, "Look! This is something new"? It was here already, long ago; it was here before our time.* (Ecclesiastes 1:9-10, NIV)

God's Word is not outdated and it never leaves out anything we need to know. Second Peter 1:3-4 tells us that we have everything we need for all of life and how to be a godly man or woman found in the precious promises of the Bible.

. . . seeing that His divine power has granted to us everything pertaining to life and godliness, through the true knowledge of Him who called us by His own glory and excellence. For by these He has granted to us His precious and magnificent promises, so that by them you may become partakers of the divine nature, having escaped the corruption that is in the world by lust.

By getting to know the Lord Jesus Christ intimately through His Word and our living obediently to Him, we can come to know all we need to know for every issue of life. And that will never change.

As we read through this short Hebrew story of Ruth, we are immediately impressed with one stark fact; these are real people living their lives on a day-to-day basis. They felt joy and they suffered great loss. They were excited and they were discouraged. They knew what it is to have made a big mistake and then have to "come home to face the music." They experienced despair and they found hope.

In fact, these are real people facing similar situations that you and I face today. They were no different than we are now.

A second thing we see is that the issues they faced are similar to the issues that we face. They struggled with the death of a family member, loss of hope for the future, despair over a dismal present, much more. Sometimes they lived in abundance and sometimes it was a struggle to put food on the table. Neither the passing of time nor the differences of culture will erase the common struggles of life. They are the same the world over.

Third, beyond real people facing real issues, we see the Bible giving Naomi, Ruth, and Boaz real answers to the issues they faced. We also see the sovereignty of God in directing the lives of His people, even when they have gone astray and are not living obedient to His Word. We see Him directing their lives back to the life He had planned for them in ways that are beyond their wildest imaginations. We see Him saying "Trust Me," even when times do not look good. Through it all He was working on their behalf. We see Him providing for their daily needs when they were helpless. We see Him faithful to His Word as they sought to live their lives based upon the principles of the Word of God (and how He rewarded them for doing it).

In John 6:29, the Bible tells us, *"Jesus answered and said to them, 'This is the work of God, that you believe in Him whom He has sent.'"* Everything that God does to us and for us and in us and around us is designed to enable us to place absolute confidence and faith in the person and work of the Lord Jesus Christ. He is always at work in our lives stretching our faith so that we will come to know Him more personally through our experiences and learn to trust Him more fully.

One thing stands out above all else. We see that life is all about Jesus. For in the end, Ruth had a son, who became the grandfather of David, whose lineage centuries later, gave us the Lord Jesus Christ. Ruth and Boaz unknowingly played an integral part in bringing about the human lineage of Jesus. And it is just like you and me, our lives are to be all about Jesus — living for Him, doing His will, obeying His Word, and preparing one day to stand before Him and give an account for all we have done, or failed to do. Life for us is like life for Ruth — ultimately, it is all about Jesus.

So the book of Ruth is about real people, like us, who face real issues, like we face, and real answers on how to live. It is a power packed book that can change our lives as we also struggle with our day-to-day life. We too can get direction for the issues we face from God through His Word and through His Holy Spirit.

In Proverbs 25:2, the Bible says, *It is the glory of God to conceal a matter, but the glory of kings is to search out a matter.* I often wondered about that verse until I came across Deuteronomy 17:18-20 that gives instructions about what a King of Israel was to do when he first ascended to the Throne:

Now it shall come about when he sits on the throne of his kingdom, he shall write for himself a copy of this law *on a scroll in the presence of the Levitical priests. It shall be with him and he shall read it all the days of his life, that he may learn to fear the L*ORD *his God, by carefully observing all the words of this law and these statutes, that his heart may not be lifted up above his countrymen and that he may not turn aside from the commandment, to the right or the left, so that he and his sons may continue long in his kingdom in the midst of Israel.*

The new King of Israel was to sit in the presence of the priests and copy by hand the Bible as they had it then. That meant that the King was the only one who had a personal copy of the Word of God; the priests did not have their own copy — it was the copy for the Temple or for the Tabernacle — but it was not their own personal copy. Only the King had a personal copy of God's Word. Not like today when every believer can have a personal copy of God's Word. On my computer, I have a Bible program that includes twenty-one different versions of Bible and about that many hard copies of the Bibles on my bookshelves. But in the Old Testament times, it was not so.

So if we go back to Proverbs 25:2, we can paraphrase it to say in today's language that *"it is glory for God to conceal a matter, but it is the glory of anyone who has a personal copy of the Word of God to search it out."*

Finding a new truth in the Bible is very much like an Easter egg hunt. Parents work hard with great anticipation to hide the chocolate figures and the assorted candies in the area reserved for the hunt. Some are hid fairly openly and others take more time and energy. They are excited to hide the candies in hopes of seeing the children find them. Then when the children actually do find the candies that have been hidden for them, the children get excited at what they have found. They hold up their candy and shout, "I found it! I found it!" Then they scamper off with new excitement to find other hidden treasures. It brings joy to the parents who have hidden the candies for the children to find. They enjoy seeing the excitement in the children as they find the chocolate treasures.

In the same way, God has hidden great, golden nuggets of truth in His Word; things that we cannot see by a casual reading of the text. When we dig into the Word of God and ask the Holy Spirit to uncover hidden truths, then He reveals them as we study with a pure heart. It then brings joy to our hearts as we uncover them. We, then in turn, bring joy to the heart of our heavenly Father when we come to learn these precious truths that He has hidden in His Word for us to find.

My hope is that you will uncover hidden truth in His Word as you dig deep into the book of Ruth and allow the Holy Spirit to reveal His treasures to you. So get out your Bible, grab a pen and a notebook, put on your running shoes, and let's dig in.

Introduction to the Story of Ruth

The book of Ruth is a Hebrew short story that is composed of six different scenes and an epilogue containing the lineage of the tribe of Judah from Genesis 49:8-12 up to King David. Each scene has a unique emphasis and covers a different time frame.

Scene One: (Ruth 1:1-5) "The Myth of the Greener Grass." This story covers a time period of a little more than ten years. Elimelech and Naomi had taken their family to the neighboring country of Moab to escape the famine in Bethlehem. They had left the land of God's promise to go to Moab where the enemies of God lived. While they lived in Moab, their two sons married Moabites.

This scene sets the stage for the remainder of the book.

Scene Two: (Ruth 1:6-22) "Coming Home to Face the Music." This story covers the approximate six week journey from Moab to Bethlehem. Naomi came back to her home a different woman. Life in Moab had drastically changed her. In this scene we see two things that were a demonstration of God's kindness and grace to Naomi. First, Naomi returned at exactly the perfect time — the time of the beginning of the harvest season. Second, God's provision of Ruth, Naomi's daughter-in-law, would prove to be a blessing of lifetime provision for Naomi and her means of return to social standing in Bethlehem. All of this was done under the sovereign hand of God.

Scene Three: (Ruth 2:1-23) "God's Unfailing Faithfulness to His People." In this scene, the sovereign hand of God directed Ruth to a field belonging to Boaz, Naomi's close relative. Ruth is allowed to glean in Boaz's field and he begins to assume a role of provision and protection over her. At this point Naomi's despair turns to hope. This scene covers the approximate seven weeks of harvest.

Scene Four: (Ruth 3:1-18) "A Night to Remember." This scene is a pivotal account of the lives of Ruth and Boaz during one impor-tant night. It covers the time from the end of the harvest celebration to early morning — about 6 to 8 hours.

Scene Five: (Ruth 4:1-12) "A Man on a Mission." In this scene is the account of Boaz acting on the principles of Scripture to invoke his right and privilege as a kinsman redeemer and the right to marry Ruth. Boaz knew what he had to do and he set out to do it. It covers the activities of the one morning following scene four.

Scene Six: (Ruth 4:13-17) "Make Lemonade When God Hands You Lemons." This scene covers the events of at least one year after Boaz was given the role of the kinsman redeemer. It shows how trusting in the Lord God can make great joy out of a seemingly hopeless situation. It is a vivid demonstration of how God can take a bad situation, even an evil situation, and turn it into a blessing if we will allow Him to do it (Genesis 50:20).

The Epilogue: (Ruth 4:18-22) "Life Goes on Generation after Generation." The closing story covers a period of 900 years. It shows us in a snapshot form, the resulting actions of how the Lord God used everything to bring about His working in the unfolding drama of His plan for the ages.

Who Wrote the Book?

The author of the book of Ruth does not identify himself within the writing of the book, nor does any other book of the Bible mention who the author could have been. The Jewish teachings in the Talmud suggest that Samuel wrote the book, however two factors are against this position. First, the literary style of the Hebrew language is not the same as the literary style that as found in the books of 1 & 2 Samuel. Language changes over the course of time and the style of writing within the book of Ruth suggests a later style such as during the time of the united monarchy in Israel's history. Second, the author of Ruth mentions David in the lineage of the tribe of Judah and the significance was that David could fulfill the promise given to Judah (Genesis 49:10) that his descendants would rule over Israel. However, Samuel died before David was crowned King of Israel (1 Samuel 25:1). He could have written under the inspiration of the Holy Spirit about things that happened after his death, but coupled with the first exception mentioned above, it is not likely. A second possibility about the author of the book of Ruth is that Isaiah wrote it, but again that is only specula-tion. However, it is most commonly accepted that Isaiah was indeed the author of the book of Ruth.

When Was Ruth's Book Written?

The book of Ruth was probably written during the reign of David since Solomon's name is not mentioned in the genealogies at the end of the book. Also in dating the book, it was mentioned that the setting of Ruth was "during the time of the judges" (1:1). Additionally it was said of the procedure of taking off the shoe to break the responsibility of a kinsman redeemer was something that was "the custom in former times," (Ruth 4:7) meaning the time of the writing was much later than the setting.

Some Important Reasons for the Book of Ruth

There are at least five major reasons that the book of Ruth was given to us as part of the written Word of God.

First, the book of Ruth establishes the fact of God's desire that all people know Him and walk with Him, including the Gentiles. This is not just a New Testament concept, but is throughout the Biblical record. God has always wanted even those who considered themselves to be His enemies to come to know Him and to live for Him. The Apostle Paul reminds us the before we were reconciled to God, we also were enemies of His.

For if while we were enemies we were reconciled to God through the death of His Son, much more, having been reconciled, we shall be saved by His life. And not only this, but we also exult in God through our Lord Jesus Christ, through whom we have now received the reconciliation. (Romans 5:10-11)

Second, the book of Ruth demonstrates the sovereignty of God as He orchestrates the everyday events and the lives of the people of the story. This He did while Naomi was not living her life in obedience to Him and Ruth was just a new believer. If He sovereignly guided their lives, how much more so can He guide one who knows Him and is living in obedience to Him and His Word?

Third, to show that even during a time of national apostasy during the times of the judges (Judges 21:25), there still was a remnant of people who acknowledged the Lord God and lived for Him in their daily lives, such as Boaz did. Paul tells us in Romans 12:2, we need not let our lives be conformed to the ways of the world system; instead, we are to be transformed by reading God's Word and walking in daily obedience to Him. This is what Ruth and Boaz did and it is what we are to do as well.

Fourth, the book of Ruth demonstrates the concept of the kinsman-redeemer with Boaz becoming a type of Jesus Christ, our Kinsman-Redeemer. This teaching of the Kinsman-Redeemer is recorded only one other time in the scriptures with negative implications (Genesis 38:6-10), but Boaz alone correctly demonstrated how it is to work out in practical, everyday living of God's people.

Fifth, the final verses of Ruth were the only written record that was available at the time of its being written that connected the family of David with the tribe of Judah; in 1 Samuel, David is known merely as "the son of Jesse." The intentions of the author were not to give a complete record of David's ancestors, but to give a biographical sketch of David's family background. Without the book of Ruth, David's right to sit upon the throne of Israel would have been held in question.

Why It Is Where It Is

Few people have ever read the book of Ruth. Yet many of those who have read it have missed its real meaning. Focusing only upon the love story of Ruth and Boaz they have missed the book's deeper significance.

It is understood that from the early rabbinical scholars, who placed the books in their present order, that they considered the primary value of the book of Ruth to be more than a mere love story. Had it been so considered they would have placed Ruth in the "writing" section of the Scriptures along with Job, Psalms, Proverbs, Ecclesiastes, and the Song of Solomon. But, because they considered the primary purpose of the book of Ruth to be historical, it has been consistently placed where it is today — with the historical books of the Bible (Joshua, Judges, 1 & 2 Samuel, 1 & 2 Kings, and 1 & 2 Chronicles).

A *Prayer as We Begin*

As we begin our study of the book of Ruth, I pray that the lyrics of this modern day hymn, *Ancient Words*[1], will be our prayer.

Holy words long preserved
for our walk in this world,
They resound with God's own heart
Oh, let the Ancient words impart.
Words of Life, words of Hope
Give us strength, help us cope
In this world, where'er we roam
Ancient words will guide us Home.

CHORUS:
Ancient words ever true
Changing me, and changing you.
We have come with open hearts
Oh let the ancient words impart.

Holy words of our Faith
Handed down to this age.

---

[1] Words and music by Lynn DeShazo © 2001 Integrity's Hosanna! Music

Came to us through sacrifice

Oh heed the faithful words of Christ.

Martyrs' blood stains each page

They have died for this faith

Hear them cry through the years,

Heed these words and hold them dear!

CHORUS:

Ancient words ever true

Changing me, and changing you.

We have come with open hearts

Oh let the ancient words impart.

Scene #1

The Myth of the Greener Grass
Ruth 1:1-5

It is never good when a Believer chooses to disobey God. The result of that decision is never good and the loss is always high! The opening chapter of the book of Ruth tells us the tragic story of Elimelech's family. It is always more safe to be in the place God wants me to be, even under His hand of discipline, than to be out of the place He wants me to be. Although God is always faithful to us in our unfaithfulness, forgiveness always has continuing consequences. Our sin and God's forgiveness are like hammering a nail into a

33

board (our sin) and then pulling the nail out (God's forgiveness); the hole that remains in the board represents the continuing consequences. And yet, God will use even the "nail holes" in our lives to glorify Himself.

The book of Ruth opens with the declaration, *"Now it came about in the days when the judges governed . . ."* (Ruth 1:1). That opening statement in the book of Ruth tells us volumes of information regarding the setting of the day. The time of the judges was a time of political turmoil throughout Israel and it tells us of the prevailing attitude throughout the country. It was a time when people did not turn to the living God for their life directions, nor did they seek direction in His Word; it was just like is recorded twice in the book of judges, *"everyone did what was right in his own eyes"* (Judges 17:6 & 21:25). As we read through the book of the judges we are impressed with a cycle of living that repeats itself over and over during the 350 years of the recorded history of the time of the judges. In fact, we see this up and down cycle of Israel's history

repeated twelve times over and each cycle
consisted of the same seven characteristics.

The Seven Stages of
Israel's Sin Cycle

Stage #1: Blessing. First, there was peace
in the land. Israel was God's people and
His blessing was upon them which included
His protection, provision, and prosperity
(Deuteronomy 28:1ff). There was peace and
abundance in the land.

Stage #2: Compromise. Negligence, apathy,
and compromise are characteristic of this
second stage. Israel would either neglect
the sacrifices and offerings or merely do them
from outward traditions without any inward
spiritual meaning.

In Song of Solomon (2:15) Solomon refers
to the ". . . little foxes that spoil the vine
. . ." When the larger foxes entered into
the vineyard they ruffled the vines as they
trampled through the vineyard, destroying
the crop as they went. The vinedresser could
see the vines moving and hear them rustling

and would enter the vineyard to chase the larger foxes away. However, the little foxes could easily go under the vines undetected by the vinedresser and they could do much more damage to the vines because of their smaller size. Negligence, apathy, and compromise are like the little foxes; not necessarily big sins, but the beginning of a life that leads to greater sin.

Stage #3: Sin. After compromise, Israel fell into sin. The sin of neglect or apathy towards God always leads to sin in other areas of life. Sin never stands still; it always leads to more sin and often leads to compromises in other areas of life. In the New Testament, sin is described as being leaven, or yeast, Matthew 16:5-12 & Luke 12:1. Both represent corruption of the host in which they are found and both will permeate the whole unless they are removed completely.

When Israel neglected their God, they began to take on the characteristics of their surrounding, godless neighboring countries. This small sin at the beginning began to grow and grow until it took over their whole life. It is the same with us — we are either becoming more like Jesus (Romans 8:29) or we are becoming more like the world; there is no middle ground.

Stage #4: Chastisement. God loved Israel too much to abandon them when they sinned. He loved them so much that He often sent them some form of discipline that was designed to bring them back to a living relationship of obedience and dependence upon Him. When adversity strikes, people suddenly acknowledge God and call upon Him in prayer, even those who previously ignored Him and lived a life independent of Him. It was the love of God for His people that prompted Him to raise up a surrounding country to deliver His discipline upon Israel so that they in turn might see their sin and their neglect and their apathy towards Him and repent. Having accomplished His purposes in their lives, they called out to Him in repentance and cried out to Him for His help in their pain and suffering.

Stage #5: Repentance. Israel then recognized her sin, repented of it, and cried out to God for His help.

Stage #6: Deliverance. Upon hearing her cry for help, God raised up someone to deliver His people. That person was a regional, temporary, military leader. He or she mustered up an army and then lead Israel to defeat her enemies. That deliverer of God's people was called a "judge."

Stage #7: Victory. The final stage of Israel's seven stage sin cycle is that God gave Israel victory over her enemy. It was not because Israel had a superior army or that she was more powerful or had a better strategy than that of her enemy, it was only because God was with them and that He gave them victory.

This seven stage sin cycle was repeated twelve times during the 350 years of the Judges. This was a time of political turmoil of ups and downs, of peace and war. It was during this time that Ruth's story took place.

In Ephesians 6:12, the Apostle Paul tells us that for every situation, there are underlying causes, and visible effects.

For our struggle is not against flesh and blood, but against the rulers, against the powers, against the world forces of this darkness, against the spiritual forces of wickedness in the heavenly places.

The visible effects are seen in the conflict between *"flesh and blood,"* that is, conflicts between friends or neighbors, marriage conflicts, family conflicts, even nation against nation in war. But even though that is where the struggle is seen, the source of it is always the same — *"the spiritual forces of wickedness."* When we give opportunity for the enemy to work in our lives, he comes in and produces struggles within us and around us. It is true with us today, and it was true with Israel during the time of the Judges.

Here is a graphic of what Israel's seven stage sin cycle looked like in their national life:

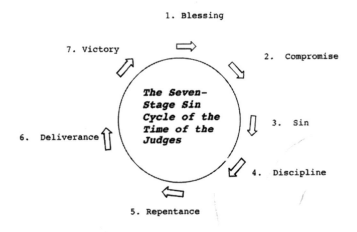

Just like Paul wrote in Ephesians 6:12, there were underlying causes for the outward turmoil that Israel was facing. Israel had failed to do two main things in her life that gave the enemy opportunity to work. First, they did not completely obey in doing what the Lord God had told them to do. Before they entered into the Promised Land, God had told them to totally defeat the inhabitants of the land (Deuteronomy 7:1-4; Joshua 11:20). However, Israel did not totally defeat her enemies; she quit before the job was finished.

Later these enemies became a constant problem often leading Israel into sin and away from her God. It is the same for us today; God requires complete obedience in our lives. Those areas of my life that I do not bring under the complete Lordship of Jesus Christ will continue to war against my soul and bring defeat to my life.

In addition to incomplete obedience, Israel had one other fatal flaw that gave the enemy opportunity to work his destructive deeds in her life. They did not live for the Lord nor did they serve the Lord wholeheartedly (Joshua 22:5; 23:6-16; Judges 3:7), instead they worshipped the false gods of the people they allowed to stay. God had told Israel that the reason they were to drive out the inhabitants of the Promised Land was because of the greatness of their sin and their prac-tices of wickedness:

Do not say in your heart when the Lord your God has driven them out before you, "Because of my righteousness the Lord has brought me in to possess this

land," but it is because of the wicked-
ness of these nations that the Lord
is dispossessing them before you. It
is not for your righteousness or for
the uprightness of your heart that you
are going to possess their land, but
it is because of the wickedness of
these nations that the Lord your God is
driving them out before you, in order
to confirm the oath which the Lord swore
to your fathers, to Abraham, Isaac and
Jacob. (Deuteronomy 9:4-5)

Israel did not completely drive out the
inhabitants of the land; they allowed them to
continue to live and to practice their evil
ways. Rather than influencing those towards
righteousness in living for the true God,
Israel began to adopt the former inhabitants' evil practices.

A lack of complete obedience and a less
than wholehearted commitment to the Lord God
will always lead to giving opportunity for
the enemy to bring disruption and conflict.
It does today and it did during the time of

the Judges. When God's people influence the world, it is called "evangelism;" when the world influences God's people, it is called "apostasy."

****

✝ Are there any areas of incomplete obedience in your life?

✝ Do you love the Lord God with your whole heart?

✝ Is there any evidence of this seven stage sin cycle in your life?

✝ What steps can you take to stop it?

****

A Famine in the Land

Ruth 1:1 also gives us another clue as to the setting of the book — *there was a famine in the land.* It seems ironic that in Bethlehem there was a famine! "Bethlehem" in the Hebrew language means "house of bread;" so in the house of bread there was no bread. God has often used famines throughout the course of human history in order to accomplish His will. He is the sovereign controller of the universe and is able to do all He desires (Romans 4:21, Numbers 23:19). In fact, there are thirteen famines mentioned in the Bible:

- In Canaan during Abraham's time — Genesis 12:10.
- In Canaan during Isaac's time — Genesis 26:1.
- In Canaan during Jacob's time — Genesis 41:54-57.
- In Israel during the time of the judges — Ruth 1:1.
- In Israel during David's time — 2 Samuel 21:1.
- In Israel during Elijah's time — 1 Kings 17:1.
- In Israel during Elisha's time — 2 Kings 4:38.
- In Samaria during Elisha's time — 2 Kings 6:25.

44

- In Israel during Elisha's time —
  2 Kings 8:1.

- In Jerusalem during Zedekiah's time —
  2 Kings 25:3 and Jeremiah 14:1.

- In Israel during Nehemiah's time —
  Nehemiah 5:3.

- In the land where the prodigal son
  lived — Luke 15:14.

- As prophesied by Agabus to occur in the
  Roman Empire — Acts 11:28.

In the Scriptures, famines were never presented as mere random acts of God; when a purpose is stated, the purpose that is most often stated is that of the judgment of God.

✝ 2 Samuel 21:1 and 24:13.

✝ 2 Kings 8:1.

✝ Psalm 105:16.

✝ Isaiah 51:19.

✝ Jeremiah 14:12, 15; 15:2; 24:10; 27:8.

✝ Ezekiel 5:11-12; 12:16.

In an agriculturally based economy, such as Israel's, a famine was devastating. However, a clue to the Israelites that this famine was sent to Israel for a purpose should have been seen in that although the famine covered the whole land of Israel, only 50 miles away in the country of Moab, there was an abundance of bread. Another such instance is found in 2 Kings 8:1-2 where there was a famine in Israel, but not in adjoining countries. God was dealing very specifically with His people. What is obvious to us in hindsight was not understood by the people of the day. Their hearts were not in harmony with the Lord or with what He wanted to do in their midst.

Going to Where the Grass was Greener

In the setting of famine and political turmoil, there was a citizen of Bethlehem named Elimelech (whose name means "my God is King"). For some unstated reason, Elimelech decided to take his family away from Bethlehem; perhaps it was to take them to a place that had less conflict and more food to eat. Elimelech had a wife named Naomi (whose name means "pleasant one") and two sons — Mahlon (his name means "sick") and Chilion (his name means "pining," which means "wasted," or "insignificant"). When Elimelech decided to take his family to Moab, it was to be only for a short time since Ruth 1:1 says he went to "sojourn" there. To sojourn in a foreign country was similar to an extended vacation; they came to enjoy the land, but did not take up residence nor did they become land owners. Like many other short term plans that become comfortable for us to live within, Elimelech's sojourn turned into a long term stay in Moab.

The Moabites were the incestuous ancestors of Lot and his oldest daughter (Genesis 19:36-37). When Israel was traveling to the Promised Land Moab refused to allow them to pass through their land. Israel had offered to stay on the straight passage through Moab and to pay for any water of food their animals consumed on the way, but Moab still refused (Deuteronomy 23:3-5 and Judges 11:17). Further, the King of Moab hired the prophet Balaam to curse Israel. It was only when Moab seduced Israel to idolatry and impurity (Numbers 25), and hired Balaam to curse them, that they were excluded from Jehovah's congregation to the tenth generation (Deuteronomy 23:3-5). This exclusion of Moab in Israel's congregation was meant to include marriages as well as intermingling with them (Nehemiah 13:1-3, 23-25 and Ezra 9:1-2).

Additionally, Lot's youngest daughter also had an incestuous relationship with him and she also had a son whom she called Ammon. Ammon became the founder of the Ammonites. Because Ammon and Moab were half brothers, the Ammonites and the Moabites are often spoken of as being inclusive with one another; when one was spoken of, it was implied that the other was also included. The two tribes were so connected that their names seem sometimes to have been used interchangeably (cf. Deuteronomy 23:3 with Numbers 22:2-7; 21:29 with Judges 11:24; and Judges 11:13 with Numbers 21:26).

In order for Elimelech to take his family to Moab, he had to violate these known commands God had place on Israel regarding mingling with Moabites. Elimelech decided to leave the Promised Land that God had given to Israel and to go live in a land that God had said to conquer, not one with which to become friendly. In doing so, Elimelech exposed himself, his wife, and his two sons to spiritually unprotected lives. Elimelech's name claimed that his "God is King," but evidently God was not King of Elimelech's life.

There was a principle of Scripture at work here, one about which Elimelech did not know. In the first two chapters of the book of Job, the Bible tells us that if a man seeks to live rightly and obediently to the Lord God, then God will build a hedge of protection around his life and all that he has — his wife, his children, and all his possessions. Then if the devil wants to in some way touch that spiritual man or anyone or anything in his care, he must first get permission from the Lord God in order to do it. Even then, if God does give the devil permission to touch the man or anything or anyone in his care, that God will do two things. First, God will limit the temptation/trial in type, length, and in intensity (Revelation 2:10 and 1 Corinthians 10:13). Second, God will in some way use that whole situation for His glory (Genesis 50:20

& Romans 8:28-29) to accomplish His purposes. But if a man voluntarily leaves that place of God's protection, as Elimelech did, then he has exposed himself and his family and his possessions to any attack of the devil because the hedge of protection has been abandoned. [NOTE: However, like Job (Job 1 & 2) and Peter (Luke 22:31-32) sometimes Satan demands permission to touch a person's life through no fault of their own; and the Lord grants his request.]

One guiding principle of the Christian life is that it is much better to be in the place God wants us to be, even under His hand of discipline, than to be out of the place God wants us to be and into a place He has told us not to enter. And when we leave the place of His blessing, He still does not desert us; He seeks to draw us back to the place where He can bless us.

Temporary Solutions with Permanent Consequences

Elimelech went to Moab intending to make it a short visit (Ruth 1:1). It was a noble cause, after all, a man has to provide for his family and there was no bread in Bethlehem, but there was in Moab. Then sometime after Elimelech and his family moved to Moab, they lost sight of their short term goal and became comfortable in the land; soon they were there to stay. But that decision that Elimelech made to live in Moab cost him his life and the lives of his two sons. Elimelech and Naomi not only became comfortable with their new home in Moab, but they allowed their two sons to marry Moabite women.

****

When a major decision needs to be made, what do you do? Do you seek the direction of the Lord in prayer? Do you seek godly counsel? Do you consider what Biblical principles may be applied to your decision? Do you have peace in your heart from the Holy Spirit?

****

Marks of a Flawed Decision-Making Process

In the decision-making process that Elimelech and Naomi used, there was no mention of either of them seeking direction from the Lord God. Their decision seems to be made entirely upon the basis of external, financial situations, or upon their feelings, or upon mere human logic.

Elimelech was an "Ephrathite" — members of the elite in Bethlehem. They were used to a higher standard of living and when hard times came, they went looking for a more comfortable place to live. When the cost was high, they did not obey the Lord God. And that is how it usually happens. When we perceive that the personal cost is too high to live a life of obedience to the Lord, we follow the path of disobedience. But when we consider the blessings of living in obedience to the Lord God, any personal cost that might be involved is very small in comparison. Further, they either ignored, or naively overlooked, the warnings of God regarding associating with Moabites from God's Word, the Bible.

Also, they had evidently grown slack in their worship of God. There was no mention of them returning to Jerusalem each year to attend the three holy days that were mandatory for all Jews — the three holy convocations of the Feasts of Unleavened Bread, the Feast of Weeks, and the Feast of Tabernacles (Deuteronomy 16:16).

Anytime we seek to make a major life decision, we must seek the Lord God in prayer and ask Him for His guidance. Proverbs 3:5-6 gives us some basic insight into this process of the Lord giving us His guidance; we need to do three things and then He will guide us. First, we need to *"Trust in the Lord with all your heart."* That is, we place our complete confidence in Him — in His Word and in His ways; we know that all He has in store for us is the best for His glory and for our benefit.

Second, we need to *"And do not lean on your own understanding."* This does not mean that living for the Lord Jesus means I do not need to be a thinking person, or that

I cannot employ my previous experiences of life applied to present understandings. It does mean that I do not trust only in my own understanding, but that I am willing and able to exercise faith in the leading of the Lord Jesus in areas I do not fully understand.

Third, receiving the guidance of the Lord means *"In all your ways acknowledge Him."* This means that I am vocal about my faith in the Lord Jesus. I am not a member of "Heaven's Secret Service." I let others know I am a Christian and I freely share how that faith in Jesus works out in the daily settings of my life.

Now if I do those three things, then I can trust in His leading my life in the path He has chosen for me; . . . *And He shall direct your paths.* It is like the rudder on a ship. When the ship is in motion, then the rudder is moved itdirects the path of the ship. But when the ship is tied to the dock, and the rudder is moved, then it only makes small waves but no direction is given. So when we do the three things listed in Proverbs 3:5-

6a, our life is in motion for the Lord Jesus and then He is able to direct my life.

The path of utter destruction is paved with self-reliance and self-sufficiency. Ever since the days of the Garden of Eden, man has been seeking to live independently of the Lord. Living automously always comes at a high cost of forfeiting His guidance in our lives and sometimes it risks enduring utter grief and tragedy.

There is no record of Elimelech seeking the Lord in prayer, or in searching out principles from the Word as to what he should do. And there is no record that he returned to Jerusalem to worship the Lord at the three times each year that was required of all Jewish men. So Elimelech took his wife and two sons and moved to Moab to escape the famine that was in Bethlehem.

But there is no where that anyone can go to escape the sovereign hand of God. David wrote in Psalm 139:7-12,

Where can I go from Your Spirit? Or where can I flee from Your presence? If

I ascend to heaven, You are there; if I take my bed in Sheol, behold, You are there. If I take the wings of the dawn, if I dwell in the remotest part of the sea, even there Your hand will lead me, and Your right hand will lay hold of me. If I say, "Surely the darkness will overwhelm me, and the light around me will be night." Even the darkness is not dark to You, and the night is as bright as the day. Darkness and light are alike to You.

There is simply no place we can go on earth, or under the earth where the Lord does not see us clearly. Even in Moab, God saw Elimelech as easily as He did in Bethlehem.

It did not take long after they arrived in Moab for Elimelech to make the transition and his short term stay that he had formerly intended gave way to a comfortable long term residence. But God intervened and Elimelech died. We might think that Naomi would have then gone back home to Bethlehem to their home they left behind, but she did not go.

Instead, she also was committed to stay in Moab and her two sons took for themselves Moabite women as wives. Her life of comfort in godless Moab overruled her obedience to Lord.

We can never escape the hand of our sovereign God. Elimelech and his family had left Bethlehem seeking to escape the famine upon the land of Israel, but ended up not being able to escape his death, and later the deaths his two sons. When running from a problem, especially a God-designed problem, the cost gets higher the longer we run. We sometimes believe a lie from the devil that we can go somewhere else and start over fresh while ignoring our current situation. Usually it is not what happens to me that impacts me the most, it is how I react to it. It was not the famine that killed Elimelech and his two sons; it was their trying to escape the hand of God's discipline.

Wrap Up

1. Consider the high cost of disobedience that Elimelech and his family endured. Imagine what would have happened if there had been obedience instead of disobedience. How much better would have things turned out if Elimelech had stayed in Bethlehem and sought the blessing of the Lord instead.

2. It is always safer to be in the place God wants me to be, even under His hand of discipline, than to leave the place He wants me to be to seek temporary relief.

3. National calamities are not random acts without divine purpose; God is the sovereign controller of the universe and He orchestrates events of human history to accomplish His will.

Scene #2

Going Home to Face the Music
Ruth 1:6-22

S everal years ago there was a commercial on
TV for a bath soap called "Calgaon." When
the pressures built up in a person's life,
they could put some of these soap crystals in
their bath water and all their worries would
shrink away in comparison to the pleasures
of the bath. In the commercial, people called
out, "Calgaon, take me away!" There are a
multitude of ways we can escape the pressures
of life, but the problem is that sooner or
later, we all have to come back to reality.
This is what happened to Naomi.

Over ten to fifteen years prior to this time, Naomi had left Judah with her husband and two sons to escape the hand of God judging Israel with a famine. Then Naomi heard that the famine was over and she had nothing to hold her back in Moab anymore, so she began the long trip home. The trip home was vastly different from the trip she had taken earlier to Moab; the trip home became a "hard pill to swallow." She was a member of the family of God, yet she had drifted far from Him and had paid a heavy price in doing so. Yet throughout it all, God was at work unknowingly in her life.

In the midst of all our sin and foolishness, God is always faithfully at work, bringing us back to the place where He can bless us the most. He did it with Naomi, and He does it today with you and me. He loves us too much to let us to continue going our own way, further and further from Himself.

****

 Can you identify with Naomi? Have you recently experienced a major life change? Have you ever drifted far from the Lord? How did He draw you back to Himself?

****

We do not normally like change. We are creatures of habit and resist it. We usually do not alter our lives unless something major happens. As a pastor, I previously thought that only followers resisted change and that leaders thrived on it. Then after many observations, I saw that even leaders resist change — that is unless the change was their idea.

There are three possible motivations that compel us to change.

> ➢ A great fear of loss.
> ➢ A hope of great gain.
> ➢ New information that causes us to rethink our position on an issue.

Why do you think Naomi changed her mind and returned to Bethlehem? She no longer had anything in Moab, but at least she had a home and family in Bethlehem. When she heard that the famine was over and that the Lord was blessing His people in Bethlehem, she immediately departed for home (1:6-7). It is doubtful that the famine had lasted the entire time that Naomi had been in Moab. God had orchestrated all the events that will be discussed later in the text and He put it in Naomi's heart to return at just the right time.

There is one more reason that a Believer makes a major change in his or her life. In the true, wayward child of God, there is always the persistent desire to go home again. Proverbs 22:6 reminds us, *Train up a child in the way he should go; even when he is old he will not depart from it.* Some come back humble and repentant, as the prodigal son did (Luke 15:11-32), some come back broken and bitter, as Naomi did, and some resist or suppress the desire and stay away. Even when we stray from the Lord God, He loves us too much to leave us there; He is always at work drawing us back into a personal, loving relationship with Himself.

Three Tests of Character (1:8-18)

God seems to test our character most when two distinctives of our life are present. First, times of great personal adversity give the best indicators of our true character. Anyone can live with an outward appearance that does not reflect their genuine inward character, but when adversity comes then the false outward appearance falls down and the real character appears. That is why Paul writes that the church needs to have conflict periodically in order that we might know who is genuinely spiritual (1 Corinthians 11:19). Anyone can act spiritual, but when adversity or conflict comes into the church, a carnal man will revert to carnal actions and a spiritual man will continue in spiritual applications. We would never know who is genuinely spiritual or who is carnal until the test of adversity takes place.

Second, times when we are alone also gives some good indicators of the true test of our character. It is what we do when we feel that no is around and no one can see what we are doing that reveals our true inner character. When others are around we will most likely restrain ourselves and not do what we really want to do. However, aloneness is the real test of our true nature.

****

How has the Lord used adversity to test your character?

What is it that you do when no is watching?

Why does the Lord test our character? After all, He already knows what we will do?

****

Now comes the test of Naomi's character (remember, Naomi's name means "pleasant-ness"). When Naomi returned to Bethlehem after going through a time of adversity, she faced a time of testing. In Naomi's limited vision she only saw God working in "good times." Sometimes we, like Naomi, have a limited view of God's work in our lives.

James 1:17 tells us, *Every good thing given and every perfect gift is from above, coming down from the Father of lights, with whom there is no variation or shifting shadow.* We must remember that everything that the Father gives us is a perfect gift and a good gift. However when those good and perfect gifts come down from the Father's hand, we sometimes tend to put new labels on them according to how enjoyable we find them to be. Those gifts we enjoy we label "good," but those gifts we do not enjoy so much we label them "bad." Sometimes the gifts God gives to us are not so enjoyable for us, but those gifts are for our spiritual life development and growth in Him. Through every good time and bad, we need to remember that all the gifts we receive from the Father's hand are "good and perfect."

In Israel during those days, there were very few jobs available to women and even fewer jobs available in rural areas such as Bethlehem. Being married was the one thing that promised security and stability for a woman's future. This was most likely the thought running through Naomi's mind as the three widowed women set off for Bethlehem. Naomi knew the probability of Moabite women finding husbands in Israel was somewhere between slim and non-existent, humanly speaking. Orpha and Ruth's chances of finding husbands and securing their futures would be much greater in Moab. Naomi must also have known about God's prohibition concerning intermarriages with the Moabites; it was a well-known command. So for either Orpha or Ruth to find a husband in Israel, they would need to find someone who disregarded God's Law.

Where Do You Find Happiness?

As the three women are on the road headed back to Bethlehem, Naomi stops and encourages Orpha and Ruth to stay in Moab. Why do you think Naomi sent them back home, to the worship of false gods? Moabites worshipped the female goddess Ashtaroth (fertility) and the male god Chemosh (war). The worship of these two gods of the Moabites, Ashtaroth and Chemosh, involved practices of immorality and the offerings of child sacrifices. She was essentially saying to them, stay here with your gods rather than come with me to Bethlehem and be exposed to the true and living God.

When Naomi spoke to the two women (1:8-9), did she revealed a value in her life? As she released them from their obligation to care for their elderly, widowed mother-in-law, did she imply that their happiness depended on people, places, and things? Happiness does depend upon the external. For the Believer, we seek the joy of the Lord, rather than happiness. Joy does not rely upon external situations, but rather upon an internal, personal relationship with the Lord God. Even in the midst of great turmoil, we can have joy, knowing He is in control, He is Lord of all, and He governs all that happens.

The Test of Orpha's Character

The first daughter-in-law, Orpha (her name means "stubbornness") seemed to believe happiness was dependent upon people, places, and things. When given the opportunity that Naomi presented to the two younger women, she returned to Moab. Orpha saw no advantage in the worship of the God of Israel over the worship of the gods of Moab. She may not have seen a strong testimony of love and devotion to the God of Israel displayed in Naomi's life. If she did see it, she did not comprehend it or she refused to accept it. Orpha had a sense of loyalty to Naomi, but when it conflicted with her sense of convenience, the loyalty to self was greater than the loyalty to Naomi so she returned to Moab.

Maybe a note of encouragement is needed here. Naomi was finally doing the right thing in returning to Bethlehem. Here lies a lesson for us as well. When you are doing the right thing, when you do what you feel the Lord wants you to do, do not be discouraged that some fall back and will not follow along with you; they probably do not have the same values you have, or they are not part of God's future plan for you.

The Test of Ruth's Character

Unlike her sister-in-law Orpha, Ruth (her name means "friendship") had a very different response to Naomi's urgings to return to Moab; Ruth clung to Naomi (1:14). When Naomi urged Ruth to go back, she refused to go and committed herself to Naomi with seven vows that she never broke.

****

Digging Deeper — Five Levels of Communication

The level at which we communicate with others around us is based upon the depth of the relationship that we have with them.

✠ For instance, those we meet casually we often speak to them with *clichés* without any real meaning. We tell the teller at the bank, or the store clerk, "Have a nice day." . . . whatever a "nice day" look like.

✠ A second level of communication is that of the *exchange of general information.* "Where do you live?" "What do you do for a living?" "Are you married?"

✠ The third level is that of asking a person for their *opinion, or what they think* on a subject. We ask people what they think on a variety of topics — politics, lifestyle practices, current trends, etc.

✠ The fourth level of communication is that of asking a person *how they feel* about a subject. This is going much deeper into a person's inner being. It speaks of how various things impact them on an emotional level.

✠ Finally, the fifth level is that of *intimacy* in communication. This is the sharing of that which is innermost for two people, their deepest thoughts, feelings, dreams, fears, and joys. It is the exchange of information about the very core of their being — what drives and motivates them to do what they do.

Levels one and two are usually descriptive of strangers or people whom we have just met. Level three is that of a new friend, while level four is reserved for our best friend. There are very few people who are on level five, usually only one or two; this level is the goal for every married couple to reach with their spouse and it takes years to develop.

****

The manner in which Ruth spoke to Naomi indicted that the two women had a deep and solid personal relationship with each other. Ruth's commitments came from her heart — it was communication from the fifth level. After Naomi heard Ruth make these seven vows, she never again urged her to leave her side. These seven vows are sometimes spoken of during a wedding ceremony, but I am afraid they are spoken with a mere surface understanding. What are these seven vows?

❖ **The vow of loyalty** — *"do not urge me to leave you or to turn back from following you"* Loyalty is standing with someone in his or her need, through good times and bad, even at personal cost. Ruth gave up everything in order to go with her elderly mother-in-law, Naomi. Ruth gave up her country, her family, her customs, her friends, her potential for remarriage and therefore, her potential for children. She gave it all up voluntarily in order that she might follow her mother-in-law, Naomi.

❖ **The vow of companionship** — *"for where you go, I will go"* This is more than just traveling together; it is being a friend along the way and showing concern and empathy. As her companion, Ruth cared for Naomi's emotional needs. The journey and the future became easier for Naomi to face, because she had a companion to go with her.

❖ **The vow of provision** — *"and where you lodge, I will lodge"* Lodging means more than just a place to sleep; it includes food and other physical needs. Ruth proved good on this vow when the two women returned to Bethlehem. She was the one who volunteered to go out to glean in the fields in order to provide for Naomi's physical needs.

❖ **The vow of family** — *"your people shall be my people"* It is one thing for Ruth to make vows to Naomi, but it is another thing to make vows to Naomi's people — her family. Ruth was including Naomi's family members and ultimately each of the Jewish people of Israel. Her vow was first cultural, then spiritual, and now national.

❖ **The vow of consecration** — *"and your God, my God"* This is the point of Ruth's conversion; she was turning her back on the gods of the Moabites and consecrating herself to Naomi's God

— the God of Israel. In saying, *"my God,"* Ruth was making her devotion to God personal.

❖ **The vow of stability** — *"where you die, I will die, and there I will be buried"* Ruth was making her commitment until her death and then beyond. Even in her death she would not turn back; she was resolute in her determination and would not look back.

❖ **The vow of culmination** — *"Thus may the Lord do to me, and worse, if anything but death parts you and me"* This was not just a set of vows that Ruth was making for a day, or a week, or a month, or a year; it was forever. It was the culmination of all that she was and was to become. She invoked the wrath of God upon herself if she did not fulfill everything she had vowed to do.

Naomi must have seen the resolute determination in Ruth's eyes and heard in her voice the conviction of her heart. Ruth meant what she said and she would not be swayed. She was determined. These were not just things that Ruth spoke of on the spur of the moment; she had solidified her commitment to Naomi.

****

 What godly characteristics do you see demonstrated in Ruth's life that would prompt her to make such commitments to Naomi?

Is there anyone in your life to whom you have this level of commitment?

If there is no one, which of the seven commitments seem most difficult to you?

****

The Unhappy Homecoming (1:19-21)

Have you ever played the "blame game?" It starts when you do something wrong, foolish, or inconsiderate. Rather than standing up and taking personal responsibility for the action, you blame someone else for what you did. That is what Naomi did; as soon as she returned home, Naomi began to play the blame game.

After being away for over ten years, Naomi returned to Bethlehem (1:4). Because she was formerly a part of the upper level of society, Naomi was well known by the people and her arrival caused quite a stir. Several people recognized her as the two women approached the outskirts of the town and went out to greet her. Immediately the women of Bethlehem asked Naomi several questions; they probably were not quite sure that this was Naomi.

The women merely asked, "Is this Naomi?" (Ruth 1:19) With that brief question, Naomi replied with a four-fold blame on God for all that had happened to her. She said do not call me Naomi (pleasantness), but call me Mara ("bitter") because God has dealt bitterly with me. (Ruth 1:20-21).

Four times Naomi blames God for what has happened in her life. No one had forced Elimelech and Naomi to leave Bethlehem; they did it of their own free will. They had left the land of God's promise to live in a land where God had forbidden His people to live.

No one had forced them to stay in Moab in opposition to the Word of God; they did it of their own free will. No one had forced Naomi to allow her two sons to marry Moabite women in disobedience to God's Law. Yet instead of taking responsibility for her own actions, she blamed the Lord God for all her problems.

- The Almighty has dealt very bitterly with me
- I went out full, but the Lord has brought me back empty
- The Lord has witnessed against me
- The Almighty has afflicted me

At least Naomi understood that the events of her life were not just the result of random chance, but they are the out-workings of a sovereign God in the lives of His people. However, she did have a negative understanding of how God exercised His sovereignty in her own life. Instead of acknowledging with a repentant heart the fact of God's discipline upon her and her family, Naomi

⌐⌐⌐ume bitter and blamed God for everything that had happened.

****

Digging Deeper — The Development of a Bitter Spirit

The Biblical meaning of "bitter" is best seen in how it is used in other passages of the Bible. In the New American Standard Bible (Updated Version), there are 36 verses containing the word "bitter. Of those thirty-six verses, there are four basic meanings of "bitter." They are: (1) to experience anguish or misery of heart [Genesis 27:34], (2) to describe harsh servitude [Exodus 1:14], (3) a taste, either experientially or metaphorically, that provokes extreme adverse reactions [Exodus 15:13], and (4) something that is evil, hurtful or destructive [Jeremiah 2:19].

Further, there are two other passages of the Bible that describe the development of a bitter spirit:

. . . so that there will not be among you a man or woman, or family or tribe, whose heart turns away today from the Lord our God, to go and serve the gods of those nations; that there will not be among you a root bearing poisonous fruit and wormwood. (Deuteronomy 29:18)

See to it that no one comes short of the grace of God; that no root of bitterness springing up causes trouble, and by it many be defiled . . . (Hebrews 12:15)

A bitter spirit begins when God brings into a Believer's life, or allows it to happen, an adverse experience that He intends to benefit his or her spiritual development (Romans 8:28-29). In every instance, He sends His grace along with the adverse experience so that we might also receive the power and the desire to do what is right (Philippians 2:13) in His eyes. When the adverse experience comes to a person's life, they can choose to receive the grace of God to victoriously go through the experience and become more of what He desires them to be. Or, they can choose to turn away from God reject His grace, which always leads to the beginning of a bitter spirit.

Rejecting the grace of God stimulates the seed of bitterness that lies dormant in every person's heart (Jeremiah 17:9). It begins to grow, starting with a sprout (or a root) and if left unattended, it will one day produce fruit of bitterness. From the beginning, that root will bring anguish and misery of heart and place them in spiritual bondage that will lead to a life that is evil, hurtful, or destructive, both to themselves and to others around them.

So how are we to handle the adverse experiences that touch our lives? After all, these experiences are either allowed or sent by the Lord God to make us better, and not bitter.

There are three main ways in which we react incorrectly to experiences of life that we do not like. We can (1) blame others, (2) make excuses, or (3) hold it in and do nothing; none of these responses have benefits to the Christian. These three ways of responding are those that will ultimately lead people to the development of a bitter spirit.

Conversely, there are three ways we can react in a positive manner. First, we can thank God in it (1 Thessalonians 5:18). It is important to maintain an attitude of thankfulness to God in the good times and the bad. When we remember His faithfulness to us in the past, it gives us hope in the present that He will not fail us in this situation either (Deuteronomy 31:6, 8 & Hebrews 13:5). We can also thank God because it gives us the opportunity to reaffirm our status as being a member of the family of God and to entrust our life to Him, as Jesus did to the Father when He hung upon the Cross (1 Peter 2:23). Many times we feel we are isolated from the Father when adversity comes into our lives. We can also thank Him for the outcome that He will produce in us. We know He has a purpose in it for us (Romans 8:28-29). He is sovereign and He allows adversity to make us more like His Son, Jesus Christ.

A second way we can respond positively to an adverse experience is to ask ourselves if we in any way had a part in causing the adversity. The main benefit for suffering from consequences of something we caused is our learning humility in asking others for their forgiveness. If there was any part, no matter how small, of our causing the adverse experience to come into being, then we need to seek the forgiveness of the Lord God first and then the person to from whom the experience came (1 Peter 4:15). Beyond asking their forgiveness, we need to do what we can to correct the situation and then to make restitution when possible.

A third way we can respond positively is to draw upon the grace of God and allow Him to use the adverse experience to develop the fruit of the Spirit (Galatians 5:22-23) in my life, as I humbly submit to His working in my life. Hebrews 12:15 goes on to tell us that when a believer develops a bitter spirit, two consequences result. First, the development of a bitter spirit brings trouble to the one who has it. A bitter spirit troubles every aspect of a person's life — his or her spiritual, physical, mental and emotional states of being. It also affects those around him or her in a negative manner, spreading the effects of bitterness into every relationship.

In every situation when God allows or designs an adverse experience to touch our life, we have a choice to make. We can draw upon the grace of God and allow Him to do all He desires to do through it in our lives, or we can reject the grace of God and become bitter. The choice is ours to make—to draw closer to becoming a man or woman of God, or to become a person with a bitter spirit.

To ensure that we do not develop a bitter spirit, we must forgive the one who delivered the adverse experience in our life. So then how do we forgive someone that we do not want to forgive and might even feel they do not deserve our forgiveness? First and foremost is to remember that as Christians, we do not have the option of whether or not to forgive anyone for anything. Because we have been forgiven of a huge sin debt of our own, we are obligated to forgive others of their lessor sin done to us (Ephesians 4:32).

In order to picture our own huge sin debt first, consider this. Suppose you only sin three times a day—that would almost qualify you to be called a "super saint." Sin is here defined as something you did that you should not have done, or something you failed to do that you should have done. Sins done in ignorance count the same as sins done while being aware. If you only sinned three times per day, that would amount to over 1,000 times per year (1,095 to be exact). Now consider how old you are and subtract five years for a generous deduction of the age of accountability. Then take that number and multiply it by 1,000 and that is how many sins the Lord God has forgiven you. If you are thirty-five years old, He has forgiven you of 30,000 sins; if you are twenty-eight years old, He has forgiven you of 23,000 sins. So how many sins has He forgiven you, if you are a super saint of three sins per day?

Now, if He has forgiven you twenty-five to fifty thousand sins, or more, and if you are to use the pattern of how God forgave us (Ephesians 4:32), then how can we not forgive someone else of for the one or two or twenty or fifty or hundred sins they did to us?

Further, if we do not forgive others, notice what takes place in our hearts from Matthew 18:21-35:

- ✝ The Lord Jesus calls us "wicked servants" (Matthew 18:32).
- ✝ We change from being the objects of God's mercy to the objects of His anger (Matthew 18:33-34).
- ✝ We are turned over to the "torturers" of heart, soul, and body (Matthew 18:34).

Remember, granting forgiveness to someone, whether we think they deserve it or not, is really for our benefit and not so much for them — it prevents us from the three consequences above and prevents us from becoming bitter.

Keep in mind that God forgave us long before we asked Him (Romans 5:8). In fact, we were forgiven and chosen to be in Him, before the foundations of the world (Ephesians 1:4). We have no right to withhold forgiveness from anyone, for any reason.

...e rarely feel like granting forgiveness. However, that is what Christ commands us to do. It is not a matter of what I feel like or do not feel like; it is a matter of obedience or disobedience. True forgiveness comes in two phases.

The first phase is when I forgive the person as an act of my will, often in opposition to my own feelings. I do it as an act of obedience to the Lord. Each time my anger towards them arises; I forgive them over and over again. Then, over time, there will come a shifting in the heart from forgiving the person as an act of obedience to being able to see how the Lord God used that person to teach me something new from His Word, or something new about Him, or about the Christian life, or something new about my own life.

When studying Biblical forgiveness, there is another level of forgiveness to consider. What do you say to the parents of a child that was struck and killed by a drunk driver who was out on bail from a DUI? What do you say to a wife and her 4 year old son whose father was killed needlessly by men who kill

others for a living? What do you say to the
college woman who is a victim of date rape by
a man who has done it to others several times
before? Do you see the different level of
forgiveness? What do you say to the husband
who just saw his wife fatally shot by a sniper
who claimed her as his 11th victim? Unlike
those described in the previous level, there
will never come a time when we will be able
to see how the Lord God used the person who
perpetrated their evil act upon us. We still
must forgive the person who committed their
evil act because forgiveness is for our benefit, not for theirs'. And we must continue to
forgive them in order to prevent our developing a bitter spirit that will destroy us
and the ones around us. But when forgiveness
comes from the heart, the lessons we learn
will be those we have learned from the Lord
and not from the perpetrator. We will learn
about His presence in our pain, His abiding
grace, His comfort in the Holy Spirit and the
support of His people as they gather around
us, and the empowerment of certain passages
of His Word.

It is important to remember that a wound to the heart is much like a wound to the body — the deeper the wound, the longer it takes to heal. A scratch on the arm heals in a week or so, but a cut that goes all the way to the bone may take up to a year or more to heal completely.

Then in time, when we remember the offense given to us, instead of feeling the deep pain or revengeful anger (although the pain and anger will always be there in lesser degrees), we remember the blessings of the lesson we learned, then we know that we have forgiven that person from the heart — the second phase of forgiveness.

There are experiences that we would never want to go through again. However, we would not trade the lessons that we learned from our journey through them for anything in this world, even in the midst of the ongoing pain.

****

Naomi had false image of God which led to her having a warped perception of life. In her surface view, she only saw the things

that happened and did not see the underlying hand of a sovereign God orchestrating
the events of her life to draw her back to
Himself (Jeremiah 31:3). Her carnal thinking
limited her from seeing how God was actively
involved in her life.

In Psalm 103:7, the Bible reminds us that
there are always two views of life — the
things we see and the things that the Lord
God is doing behind the scenes.

*He made known His **WAYS** to Moses,*
*His **ACTS** to the sons of Israel.*
(Psalm 103:7, emphasis mine)

Some people only see the individual acts of
God, but never understand the ways of how God
works behind the scenes. That is, they only
see random situations which they are facing
without seeing how the Lord God is using
everything to stretch their faith, remove
some of the "rough edges" of their lives, or
to make them more like the Lord Jesus. When
we learn to see the way the sovereign God is
always working in unfolding His plan for the

ages, and for our life as well, then we are able to rest in His goodness knowing that He always works things out for the ultimate best in our life and for His greatest glory (Romans 8:28). God was guiding the lives of Naomi and Ruth. However, Naomi's eyes were blinded by her former disobedience and her surface view of life.

****

 Looking back, can you think of any situation in which the Lord God was guiding your life, and yet you were not aware of it at the time?

****

Let's take a deeper look at Naomi's complaints she voiced as she came home to Bethlehem.

- **"The Almighty has dealt very bitterly with me"** — that may have been true with her, but she did see that it was a consequence of her poor choices or sin? If God had dealt very "bitterly" with her, it was to draw her back to Himself and to bring her back to the place of greatest blessing in her life . . . back home to Bethlehem.

- **"I went out full, but the Lord has brought me back empty"** — that was true, Naomi went out wealthy and "high society" and the Lord had emptied her of both. It is important to remember that when the Lord empties out the things of our lives, it is only so that He can fill us with Himself and His blessings. Little did Naomi know the vast amount of blessing the Living God had for her back in Bethlehem. She indeed did come back empty, but it was so the Lord could fill her to overflowing with His blessing for all eternity.

- **"The Lord has witnessed against me"** — that was true in her life. When we walk away from the Lord and the place of His blessing, we cannot expect to be held up as an example to others. However, she did not know that her return to Bethlehem, and everything that was to follow, would reverse the witness of God. Nor did she know that for the remainder of all time Naomi would become a testimony of God's grace and blessing.

- **"The Almighty has afflicted me"** — the Lord did afflict Naomi, but not for the reasons she may have thought. She may have thought that God had been cruel to her or that He was indifferent to her pain and loss. However, all that had happened to her was a consequence of her turning away from following the Lord. More important, the Lord had used her afflictions as a means of drawing her back to Himself. Now that she had returned to Bethlehem, her affliction would be replace with blessings beyond anything she could have imagined (Ephesians 3:20-21).

These four complaints Naomi expressed against the Lord God appear in a much different light when we set them in their larger, fuller context.

The Unseen Hand of God at Work (1:22).

When Naomi returned to Bethlehem, she could not have envisioned God's gracious provision He had prepared for her through Ruth. Nor could she have known the blessings the sovereign Lord God would bring to all His true followers through the life and message of Ruth in the ages to come. Consider these things:

- ✝ Through Ruth, God had provided a daughter-in-law to be Naomi's companion for life. Ruth was said to have been better for Naomi than seven sons could have ever been (4:15).
- ✝ Through Ruth, God would provide food for Naomi to eat and be satisfied.
- ✝ Through Ruth, God would attract a kinsman redeemer who would give Naomi the security of a family.

✞ Through Ruth, God would provide a grandson which would be a great blessing for Naomi. Further, He would give her a niche in the lineage of the Lord Jesus Christ.

✞ Through Ruth, God would bring Naomi back to Himself.

✞ Through Ruth, Naomi's life took a turn and she was able to experience the Lord's goodness and grace.

A second way in which we see the unseen hand of God working in Naomi's life, was in the timing of her return. It was at just the right time that Naomi heard there was food in Bethlehem (1:6). At that particular time, God had stirred Naomi's heart to bring her back so He could begin the process of restoring her to His grace. God always does things at just the right time, like when He sent His Son, the Lord Jesus into the world. *But when the right time came . . .* (Galatians 4:4a, NLT)

The time of the beginning of the barley harvest was just the right time for Ruth and

Naomi to return to Bethlehem (1:22). Had they come before the harvest season, it would have been too early and they would have starved. Had they have come after the harvest season, Ruth would have had no opportunity to glean in Boaz's fields. This was just the right time so that God could begin to unfold the next step in His plan for them. And yet, all the while they were totally unaware of what He was doing.

That is the way life usually is for us as well. It is a daily process of walking in obedience to the Lord so He can fulfill His purposes in and through us. Often we are unaware of His orchestrating the events of our lives for His good purposes.

Think of these two major things God was accomplishing in bringing Naomi back to Bethlehem. **First,** it was through the marriage of Ruth and Boaz that Naomi had a future. **Second,** Naomi had to return with Ruth so she could be a part of the unfolding plan of God and bring about the birth of Obed, and on to the eventual birth of the Lord Jesus.

It is an amazing thing when we walk obediently with the Lord through the daily events of our lives. He is able to lead us into the paths He has chosen for us and to accomplish His will through us. Who knows what He will do through you today, and in the days to come?

Wrap Up

1. Is there anyone you know who is like Naomi, distant from the Lord, blaming Him for their circumstances, and bitter? Maybe it is a neighbor, relative, or a co-worker. They are in need for someone to come along side them, to commit themselves to them, and to help them come back home to the Lord and once again be blessed by Him. They have the desire to return, but just need someone to come along beside them and to be with them on their journey. Do you know someone that you could assume the role of their "Ruth" and help them along their way back to the Lord Jesus?

2. God is always faithful to His children, in the good times and in the bad times, when we are faithful and when we are not faithful. Through it all, He is always ready and willing for us to come back

home. Further, He is continually active in our lives to bring us back to Himself.

3. Do you ever blame God for the things that go wrong in your life? Whenever you are tempted to blame Him, you must hold on securely to these three truths.

- God is good and He can do no evil.
- God truly loves me and has my best interests in mind.
- God's goal for me is not to make me happy, but to make me godly, like His Son, Jesus Christ (Romans 8:29).

The Set of the Sails

(Ella Wheeler Wilcox, 1916)

One ship sails east
And another west
  By the selfsame winds that blow'
'Tis the set of the sails,
And not the gales,
  That tells them the way to go!
Like the winds of the sea
Are the waves of time,
  As we voyage along through life;
  'Tis the set of the soul
That determines the goal,
And not the calm or the strife!

Scene #3

God's Unfailing Faithfulness to His People Ruth 2:1-23

In John 6:29, Jesus summarized the work of God as the Father doing whatever it takes to bring us to the place where we will have total faith in the Lord Jesus Christ. All the Father allows and does is designed to enable us to place our unswerving trust in Jesus Christ and His plan for our lives as an integral part of His overall workings in the universe. This is what He constantly does for us — and this is what He was doing in the life of Naomi. He was bringing her

to a point where she would acknowledge His
faithfulness to her, even at times when she
was unfaithful to Him.

He Did It Again,
And Again . . . . .(2:1-3)

As a child of God, we can rest in two
things: (1) the presence of God is always with
us, and (2) He continually goes on before us
to prepare the way (Deuteronomy 31:8). Our
challenge is learning to trust what He is
doing, even when we cannot see Him doing what
we think He should be doing, or when it seems
as if He is not doing anything at all.

At first it was the issue of timing, God
had prompted Naomi's heart at just the right
time to bring her and Ruth back to Bethlehem
at the time of the barley harvest. At this
scene, we see the sovereign hand of God unfold
the next step in His plan for Ruth and Naomi.
God had gone on before them to provide a
kinsmen redeemer.

The content of this passage takes place
sometime after Ruth and Naomi had returned

to Naomi's former home in Bethlehem. They had settled in and now faced a dilemma. They had nothing to eat and evidently no money with which to purchase food. Somehow Ruth found out about the Jewish practice of gleaning and requested permission from Naomi to glean in the fields around the town so they could have something to eat. With Naomi's blessing, Ruth set out to glean in someone's field — anyone's field. Under the sovereign hand of God, He led her to the place He desired her to be — the fields of Boaz.

As if giving a side note, the author of Ruth tells us that Boaz happened to be family member of Elimelech's. That is a major announcement in the unfolding drama of the book. Psalm 27:23-24 (NLT) contains a precious promise for every true follower of the Lord God.

The Lord directs the steps of the godly. He delights in every detail of their lives. Though they stumble, they will never fall, for the Lord holds them by the hand.

At first it was the issue of timing under the sovereign hand of God in Naomi's life; now it is the issue of guidance in the life of Ruth. From the view on this side of heaven, it appeared as if Ruth went to Boaz's field by coincidence. However, on the spiritual side we know she was guided there by the Holy Spirit of God according to His matchless plan for her life. When a man or woman genuinely walks with the Lord with a submissive heart, nothing is left to random chance, the sovereign hand of God is upon them.

In his daily online devotional for February 11, 2009, Dr. David Jeremiah gave the following illustration concerning the sovereignty of God.[2]

Someone once described the sovereignty of God as being like an ocean liner bound for port. While it is resolutely moving toward that destination, there are passengers aboard who are free to move about as they will. They are not

[2] Dr. David Jeremiah is senior pastor of the Shadow Mountain Community Church in El Cajon, CA. See www.davidjeremiah.org

in chains. In fact, they eat, sleep, play games, read, and talk as they please. All the while, the liner is still headed toward its predetermined port. It is a picture of both freedom and sovereignty harmoniously taking place at the same time.

As children of God, each of us has the Sovereign God as ruler in our hearts. This means that no matter what happens in life and whatever decisions we make, God resides in our hearts, steering us toward an ever-fixed mark. This is a comforting truth because as humans, we don't know what's best for our lives; and though we try to make good decisions, sometimes we just make the wrong ones. It's wonderful to know that while we're busy living and learning, God is at the helm of our life working all things together for good (Romans 8:28).

****

Digging Deeper — Life is Lived on Two Planes of Reality

The reality of life being lived on two different and equal planes is a well established fact of the Bible. There is the physical side of life which we see, hear, smell, touch, and taste. Equally real is the spiritual side where the real issues of life are waged and won or lost.

Consider Deuteronomy 8:3 where Moses reminded Israel that God had created a need and then gave a provision for that need in the form of daily manna in order that they would come to know that life is lived on the physical **_and_** spiritual realms — the bread level and the Word of God level. The content of this verse is so important that it is quoted twice in the New Testament (Matthew 4:4 & Luke 4:4).

In 2 Kings 6:8-17 there is another very interesting record of this dual reality of life. The King of Aram was at war with the

King of Israel. When the King of Aram made plans concerning his battle strategies, those plans would be relayed either by angels or by the Holy Spirit to Elisha and then Elisha would pass them on to the King of Israel. When the King of Aram heard about Elisha's actions, he sent horses and chariots to surround the city of Dothan where Elisha was living. Early the next morning, Elisha's servant went outside and saw all the horses and chariots surround the city and with great fear rushed back inside the house to shake his sleeping master awake. When the servant relayed the information to Elisha, Elisha was very calm. He merely prayed and asked the Lord to open the eyes of his servant so he could see the multitude of the chariots of fire that surrounded Elisha. Elisha prayed that his servant could see not only the reality of the physical realm (King Aram's army) but also the reality of the spiritual realm (the chariots of fire — God's angelic army) as well.

In the New Testament, the Apostle Paul reminds us again of this dual nature of reality in Ephesians 6:12, where he tells us,

For our struggle is not against flesh and blood, but against the rulers, against the powers, against the world forces of this darkness, against the spiritual forces of wickedness in the heavenly places.

The "flesh and blood" level (the physical level) is not where the real struggles of life originate, but it is where they are seen and felt. The real battles of life take place "in the heavenly places" (the spiritual realm) against the "spiritual forces of wickedness."

When the battles of life are waged in the spiritual realm, it affects the issues of life in the physical realm. Therefore, it is of great necessity for every Christian to be a growing Christian and developing equally in the five disciplines of the Christian life: (1) intake of the Word of God, (2) having a living, growing, dynamic prayer life, (3) experiencing genuine fellowship with other Believers, (4) sharing the good news of salvation in Christ alone with pre-Christians, and (5) being a responsible member of their local, Bible-oriented church. If the spiritual life of the Christian is lacking, the battles in the physical realm will be lined with defeat.

We also see this interaction of the decisions made in the spiritual realm being made effective in the physical realm in chapters 1 and 2 of the book of Job. Discussions between the Lord God and the devil were played out in the physical life of Job.

When facing the total realities of life, we must consider both planes. We see the physical side of life, but we also know the Lord God is at work in the spiritual side as well. When we know He is working and He is in control of all things, then we need not fear what is happening in our world. It is interesting to note that the New Testament word that is translated "worry" or "anxious" (Philippians 4:6) means literally to have a

divided mind. When we only see the physical
side of life without also knowing the spiritual side as well, we are left to worry.

****

Knowing the sovereign hand of God is upon
our lives is a tremendous benefit of living
for the Lord Jesus. God requires a submissive
heart before Him and before the appropriate
authorities over which He has placed in my
life. If our hearts are not submissive to Him
and to those authorities whom He has placed
over us, then His focus is to break the rebel-
lion of our heart before He can guide us into
the glorious plan He has prepared for us.

****

 If God really is sovereignly
guiding my life, how then can I
be held responsible for my
actions or inactions?

****

A Divine Collision of Enormous Proportions Is About to Take Place (2:4-16)

Let's take a brief look at the lives of Boaz and Ruth at how God formed them into the man and the woman they became. Neither Boaz nor Ruth was what we could call a product of their generation. They were not ones to follow the crowd or to do what everyone else was doing. They were principled people who were committed to doing the right thing no matter what anyone else around them was doing. We need to remember this story took place when the nation of Israel was not seeking to consistently follow the ways of the Lord God. Instead, every man did that which was right in their own eyes (Judges 21:25 & 17:6).

God tells us not to be conformed to this world, but to be transformed by His Word and by His Spirit. We can only do that after we have given ourselves completely to Him as a living sacrifice for His complete ownership (Romans 12:1-2).

* *

 What is the difference between being "conformed" and being "transformed?"

* *

One of the most powerful lessons in life can be stated like this. You and I can never govern what will happen to us, but we can always govern how we will respond to the situations that we face. So it is not what happens to us that matters, it is what happens within us that is most important.

Boaz grew up in a country that was only doing what they thought was right in their own eyes, yet he became a man who lived by the principles of the Word of God. Ruth grew up in a country that was despised by God and they ignored God in return, yet her heart was open to Him and she became a woman who could be guided by His Holy Spirit.

We do not have to be like everyone else, we also can be men and women through whom

God can work and unfold His plan in us and through us. We cannot have lives that will influence others towards saving faith in Jesus Christ, if our lives are lived no different than anyone else's. We can either live for eternity or we can live for the here and now, but we cannot do both.

****

 When do you feel pulled in two directions . . . towards the world and towards obedience to the Lord?

How do you choose what to do?

What resources are available to help you make a wise choice?

****

The Molding of a Man of the Word

Boaz was said to be a *man of great wealth* (2:1); but the Hebrew word used here and translated *wealth* could more fully mean "*resources*" — resources including other than, but might also include, money. More fully, it means that he was a man of virtue and valor, of moral and physical strength; he was a man of character and substance. It usually implied he was a man of such standing as to have his own army or employed a large work force.

A second thing about Boaz was that he was **a** kinsman redeemer, not the only one, nor the first one, but a kinsman redeemer nonetheless.

****

Digging Deeper — The Kinsman Redeemer

Although the term "kinsman" is used only seven times in the Bible (all in the Book of Ruth) and "avenger of blood" is used twelve times throughout the Bible, the Hebrew verb **go'el,** from which both of these terms are translated, is used over 100 times and rendered by such additional terms as "redeemer" or "near relative."

Since an Israelite could sell himself, his family, or his land (Leviticus 25:39-43) in cases of poverty, the kinsman (Leviticus 25:25) was provided to protect the extended family clan. This person, a near relative, had the first option by law to buy any land being sold, thus allowing it to be kept within the family clan (Leviticus 25:23-28; Jeremiah 32:6-10). Thus the kinsman role became commonly known as the "Kinsman Redeemer" because he was a close relative who would redeem the family's land.

In Naomi's case, she must have sold the land prior to her coming home. For over ten years their family lived in Moab with no stated means of income. Most likely that by the time she returned home that she still owned the family house, but the land had been sold. Also, Ruth represented another part of the redemption of the land. Since she had come home with Naomi, and Ruth had no children of her own, who ever redeemed the land was also obligated to marry Ruth and raise up children in the name of her dead husband, Mahlon. In the Old Testament the word kinsman most often is understood to mean, "One who has the right to redeem."

In the New Testament, Jesus is described as our brother (Hebrews 2:11-12, 17), who redeems us from the power of sin. Thus Boaz is presented as an Old Testament illustration of Jesus who is the New Testament fulfillment of the kinsman redeemer.

****

Boaz was a man who was in close, personal contact with the people who worked for him; he often traveled from his home to visit the workers in his fields. In a time of national moral decadence, Boaz was a man who carried his relationship with the Lord God into his workplace. His greeting carried the blessing of the Lord to those who worked for him; and they responded with mutual respect and a return blessing of the Lord upon him. *Now behold, Boaz came from Bethlehem and said to the reapers, "May the Lord be with you." And they said to him, "May the Lord bless you." (Ruth 2:4)*

That was a common greeting at that time between godly men and their servants in Israel. Think about this for a while, the employer asked for God's presence and protection for the workers as they worked in his fields. The workers would, in reply, ask God to enable their employer to enjoy the harvest of his field and to have wisdom to use his new grain for the glory of God. What would that do to labor/management relations today if work was carried out under that type of mutual respect and concern? Another example of this greeting is found also in Psalm 129:8.

Nor do those who pass by say, "The blessing of the Lord be upon you; we bless you in the name of the Lord.

Boaz's knowledge of those who worked for him was so keen that he could immediately spot someone who did not work for him. After he greeted his employees, Boaz looked out over his fields and it was then that he saw a woman that He did not know, nor had he ever seen her in his fields before.

Take notice of Boaz's first reaction to Ruth. Boaz's first concern for Ruth was not to take advantage of her, but to inquire who her protector was. From the beginning, God has placed over every woman a husband or a father (Genesis 3:16 and Numbers 30:1-16) to be a protection for her and provide for her. As both husband and wife live under that God-given protection, she is to be cared for as both of them walk in humble submission to the Lord God (1 Peter 3:7). If there is no husband, the responsibility to protect and to provide for her falls upon the father. If there is no father, then the responsibility falls upon the eldest son in the family or other men within the immediate family. Although this is the Biblical pattern, in reality, things do not always work out this way.

The Apostle Paul goes further in how widows are to be cared for in New Testament times and onward to today. First Timothy, chapter five, gives us four classes of widows and who was responsible for their protection and provision.

- Any widow who has children or grand-children was to be cared for by those children or grandchildren (5:4).
- Any younger widow who has parents who are still living is to return to their care (5:4).
  - A widow who meets the following qualifications was to be cared for by the church (5:10):
  - She does not have any near family members living
  - She is over 60 years of age
  - She was the wife of one husband
  - She gave her life to the service of the Lord and of His people

- A widow who was under 60 years of age and who had no family members alive, was to remarry and be cared for and protected by her new husband (5:11-14).

In all these situations, God's concern is for the care and provision for all classes of widows by the appropriate authorities in their lives.

****

Has there been a time in your life when you were experiencing some difficulty and God met your needs through the Body of Christ or a fellow believer?

****

The overseer of the field and the other reapers had previously met Ruth when she came to inquire about her being able to glean in the fields. They knew her and had observed her working habits, but Boaz did not know her. By this time, Ruth's reputation and character was well known throughout the community of Bethlehem. Boaz had heard of Ruth, but he evidently had not connected Ruth's reputation with the new woman he saw in his field.

A positive reputation is developed when people consistently see admirable qualities being displayed. There is a big difference between our reputation and our character. Basically, our reputation is what people think of us and our character is what God thinks of us. Also, we have no control over our reputation, but we have absolute control over our character. People will think about us whatever they want to think, but we can govern what the Lord God knows we really are. Our character is what is developed when we are committed to (1) doing what is right even when no one is watching or (2) when we know we will not receive the credit for doing what we do, or (3) when we must pay a high price to do what is right.

At the time of the mid day meal, Ruth joined the other gleaners in the field house to rest and eat some of the grain that she had gleaned that morning. The field house was a temporary shelter erected adjacent to the field that was currently being harvested. The purpose of this house was to give shade to the workers during their break times and during their meal times. The building of this field house was another expression of the practical means of concern that Boaz had for the welfare of his workers; he did not have to build such a resting place for them, but he did.

Boaz had heard about the character of the Moabite woman who had come back to Bethlehem with Naomi and he wanted to reward her for that; it takes a person of godly character to appreciate the godly character of another. Boaz had heard about Ruth's conversion to the God of Israel and about her leaving her homeland to take care of Naomi. He probably had also heard about her hard work in providing for the physical needs of Naomi.

Now, upon finding out who the woman was and then connecting this woman with the information he had heard about her, Boaz took another noble step in regards to Ruth. Knowing that Ruth had no protector, Boaz assumed the role of her temporary protector for her safety. Boaz gave a six fold charge to Ruth.

- **Listen carefully to me, my daughter.** It was a charge to listen to him only, as a daughter would to her father. There seemed to be a noticeable age differ-ence between Ruth and Boaz.

- **Do not go to glean in another field.** Boaz's protection could only be extended over Ruth within the boundaries of his own property.

- **Do not go from this one, but stay here with my maids.** There is always strength in numbers. Besides, the other maids could supply companionship to Ruth and help her throughout the day as she learned how to glean in the fields.

- **Let your eyes be on the field which they reap, and go after them.** As the harvesting servants moved from one field to another that Boaz owned, the maids would follow after them and Ruth was to follow after them as well since she was unaware of the extent of Boaz's fields.

- **I have commanded the servants not to touch you.** Ruth was very beautiful and could have had the affections of any of the young men of Bethlehem (3:10). They were not to tease her or to take advantage of her in anyway. They may have thought she was just a Moabitess far from her home and she had no one to protect her. So whether their intentions were honorable or less than honorable, the young men were commanded to leave her alone.

- **When you are thirsty, go to the water jars and drink from what the servants draw.** Ruth was elevated from that of a poor woman who was gleaning in the fields of Boaz to that of one who was under the direct care of Boaz and his servants. The command to give her water when she was thirsty was understood to mean his servants were to give her not only water, but anything she needed.

Boaz also made provisions for Ruth's food supply. When it came time for their lunch, Boaz had Ruth sit with his workers, not with the other people who were gleaning in his field. His employees were fed prepared food while the other gleaners ate of the grain they picked up that morning. Further, Boaz served Ruth her food and he gave her more than enough food for her lunch. He gave her so much that she was able to take some home in a "doggie bag" for Naomi. This showed that Ruth cared for Naomi and was thinking of her as well. While Ruth had plenty, she remembered that Naomi home with nothing to eat.

After lunch was over and Ruth had returned to her gleaning in the field, Boaz personally instructed his workers concerning her. He added intensity to his instructions by the fact that he delivered them personally to his workers, rather than having his overseer do it for him. Not only was Ruth allowed to glean, as provided by the Levitical Law, but Boaz also told his servants to allow Ruth to pick from the sheaves as well. Further, he instructed the men to purposefully drop some grain in her path. Wherever Ruth gleaned, the men were not to do anything that would embarrass her nor were they to insult her at all.

Boaz went far beyond what was required of him by the Law for gleaning, probably because he knew of the sacrifices that Ruth had made for Naomi. In this way he showed his generosity and care for Ruth as his way of rewarding her for what she had done. Kindness is never seen when we only do what is required of us. It should be noted that Boaz's actions to be Ruth's protector and her provider were noble and virtuous; they were not aimed at winning her affections. It is clear from Ruth 3:10 that Boaz did not think he was even in the running for Ruth's affections since he said he thought she could go after any of the young men, and because he knew he was not the closest kinsman to her. His motives for what he did seem to be in response to meeting the needs of this young woman.

The Molding of a Woman of the Word

Ruth was the younger, and thus the stronger of the two women, yet she submitted to Naomi and sought her permission to go work in the fields for food. Although it was a provision of the Law (Leviticus 19:9-10, Leviticus 23:22, and Deuteronomy 24:19) for her to glean the fields, she still sought permission from the servant in charge to do so. Ruth did not come as one demanding her rights, but as one who was seeking permission from those in authority over the fields.

* *

 How do you think Ruth found out about this provision of the Levitical Law?

* *

Gleaning is an Old Testament example of what we commonly call "workfare" today. It was to be a provision for the poor to work for their food without merely giving them a handout. It provided for the needs of the poor without taking away their dignity. Merely giving out money to one who could work demeans their character and diminishes their work ethic. By requiring involvement and self-effort along with the provisions, provides for their needs while building their character. Additionally, gleaning was a temporary help where as the welfare system of today most often becomes a way of life for generations in a downward spiral to hopelessness.

Ruth proved to be a hard worker, not expecting, nor demanding that the world owed her a living. Even though field work was hard, Ruth worked faithfully and diligently all day long. Her work ethic was a testimony to her character. Further, Ruth did not presume upon Boaz's attraction to demand special favors from his employees. Instead, Ruth remained focused and faithful to Naomi in providing for her food.

Success and notoriety often change people's personalities drastically. However, in view of all that the Lord God had opened up for her, Ruth continued to live with Naomi and be submissive to her. She could have "taken over" and been a woman "in charge," but she did not let her newfound status go to her head. After all, Boaz had elevated Ruth in the eyes of all his servants as well as to Ruth herself. She could have used her newfound position of favor to slack off in her work, but she did not.

Sometimes those who possess the characteristics that the culture uses to define
beauty or handsomeness think they are a valu-
able person merely because of those cultural
characteristics they possess. But when age
comes and those characteristics fade, they
feel their worth as an individual also fades.
Ruth knew her strongest asset was not her
great physical beauty, but her godly character that was developing within her.

Naomi Has Renewed Hope (2:17-23)

Remember, God is always working in the
life of the Believer, even when we don't see
evidence of it. It is at this time that the
Lord began to openly reveal Himself to Naomi
as she saw how He had directed Ruth in her
gleaning (Ruth 2:19-21). When Naomi noticed
the grain that Ruth brought home she saw
the blessing of God's provision. This is the
first time in the book that Naomi said something spiritual. Naomi knew that the amount
of food that Ruth had returned with was much
more than normal . . . it was an abundance.

The Lord God had blessed Ruth's work indeed (Ephesians 3:20-21).

An ephah was a measurement equal to about five gallons of dry goods, or about .625 of a bushel. The weight of the grain was probably about 50 lbs, an amount which might have been too heavy for Ruth to carry. In view of Boaz's charge to his servants to meet Ruth's needs, it may have been that one of the young men carried it home for her. The quantity of grain that Ruth brought home that day was by far more than any gleaner would have normally picked up during a regular day's work.

Further, when Ruth told Naomi that she had worked in Boaz's field all day, Naomi's mind immediately fast forwarded to the possibility of Boaz marrying Ruth, the stability of a family once again, and even future grandchildren — all these possibilities came to her in a split second. Naomi had knowledge of the customs of the people of Israel and of the Law of the Kinsman Redeemer, and of Boaz's relationship to her family. Naomi interpreted Boaz's generosity towards Ruth as a sign that he had more than a casual interest in her;

Boaz's interest in Ruth was probably that of a father/daughter relationship, but Naomi saw it as a potential husband/wife relationship.

The harvest season began with barley and ended with the harvest of fruits (2 Samuel 21:9) and the whole season normally lasted approximately seven weeks. The harvest season then concluded with the Feast of Weeks (Leviticus 23:15-21 and Deuteronomy 16:9-12). The times of harvest — of barley, wheat, and fruits — were times associated with the major feasts of Israel. The feasts of the Passover, First-Fruits, and Unleavened Bread were in the spring in conjunction with the barley harvest, which was the first of the harvests in Israel — Leviticus 23:4-15. The feast of Pentecost was then held seven weeks later at the conclusion of the wheat harvest — Exodus 34:22 & Leviticus 23:15-22. This was a time of the year that contained periods of great celebration and thanksgiving to God.

***

****

Digging Deeper — The Reading of the Book of Ruth

 Jewish tradition tells us that the book of Ruth was always read at some point throughout the celebrations towards the end of the wheat harvest as a part of the feast of Pentecost.

****

Because Naomi saw how God had directed Ruth thus far, Naomi was able to wait patiently for God to take them to the next step. Nothing builds hope and trust in the Lord for the future direction of our life like being able to see previous steps that were orchestrated by the Lord. Faith builds bigger faith. Day after day for about seven weeks, Ruth went to the fields to glean, but harvest time was coming to a close. Naomi waited patiently for the right time to implement her plan.

* *

 How does seeing God's guidance in the past give you hope and direction for tomorrow?

* *

The Character of Ruth After Her Relationship With Boaz.

"And she lived with her mother-in-law" (Ruth 2:23). Sometimes people change when they come into a new relationship. Not so with Ruth, she continued to be the same woman as she was before she knew Boaz. She trusted Naomi to direct her life and she remained at home throughout the harvest season, not out prowling for a husband. She could have thought that if Boaz noticed her, other men would also notice her. She also remained under the care and protection of Boaz and his maidens. She did not let her growing relationship with Boaz fill her with pride, but remained humble and submissive.

132

Wrap Up

1. The reasons God could direct Ruth in such a dynamic manner was because:

    • She had a heart to seek the Lord God (2:12).

    • She was submissive to the human authorities God had placed over her (2:2, 7).

    • She placed a higher priority of her developing godly character over her appearance (2:13).

    • She acted in faith upon the Word of God she knew (2:2, 7).

2. The reasons God could direct Boaz in such a dynamic manner was because:

    • Boaz did not let the world around him dictate his lifestyle and his behavior.

    • He was a man of godly character and he respected others of godly character.

- He did not let his influence come from his wealth, but from doing what was right before the Lord.
- He was a man whose relationship with the Lord extended to all facets of his life, especially to his workplace and to those with whom he worked.

3. How easily is God able to direct you?

- The one major point from Ruth, chapter two is this: If I want God to really direct my life then I must be a man or woman of God whose life is permeated with my relationship with the Lord God.
- What can you do that it would make it easier for God to direct you?

Scene #4

A Night to Remember
Ruth 3:1-18

There is a big difference between faith and foolishness. When we read the things Ruth did in this scene, we know Ruth acted in faith and God rewarded her for it. And her faith was not blind faith, it was Biblical faith.

Some Things to Consider First in this Chapter

We must read this scene seeking to understand first of all what was in the heart of the author that he was communicating to the mind of the original reader. We must also seek to understand the assumptions he was making about the knowledge of the original readers. Never forget that the Bible is not a western book and we cannot use a western mind to understand its meaning. We need to get our mind into the mind of those to whom it was originally intended in order to understand what they understood.

Parents arranging marriages for their child was the normal experience of the day. Often parents would make agreements with other parents about the marriage of their children and they would agree on the arrangements. Sometimes this took place long before their children were of the marrying age. Then at a time determined by the parents, the actual wedding ceremony would take place; but all the while the agreement of the parents was in place, the children were considered to have been married, even though no physical union had taken place nor had they lived together in the same house.

A second thing in the minds of the original readers was that a husband for Ruth was necessary if Naomi was to have any retirement benefits.

There were no retirement benefits afforded the people and it was the responsibility of the eldest son to provide for the future welfare of the parents until their death. If a parent had no surviving son or daughter, they had no future provision for their latter years.

****

 There seems to have been, and still are, three different ways in which marriage partners are selected: (1) marriages arranged by the parents, (2) love marriages which result from dating or courtship whereby the individuals to be married make the decisions, and (3) a combination that is an arranged marriage in which the children to be married both reserve "veto" rights over the parents' decision.

Which one do you think is practiced most in your culture?

Which one do you think is most successful?

Which one do you think is the most Biblical?

****

Naomi Has a Plan!

Why did Naomi tell Ruth to take the actions that she did (3:1-5)? The Levirate marriage law (Deuteronomy 25:5-10) was now the motivating Scripture for Naomi. This act of Naomi's indicates she had made a major shift in her life. Previous actions taken in her life were in opposition to the Word of God, but now she was acting in faith upon the principles of the Word of God.

All during the time following Naomi and Ruth's return to Bethlehem, the one who was the first in line to be the kinsman redeemer had not made any overtures towards fulfilling his obligations as a kinsman redeemer or his obligations to Ruth. The Levirate marriage law stated that if the first in line did not fulfill his responsibilities, then the wife was to take the next step. Although the first in line had not taken any interest in Ruth, the second in line (Boaz) had noticed her and had taken her under his protective care.

The Plan was Set in Motion

Naomi wanted to seek a husband for Ruth, and thus provide a secure future for herself as well. Ruth had worked hard in the fields gleaning grain for her and for Naomi, but now the harvest was over and her source of income and food was no longer available; her future was still not secure. It was the hope of every woman in Israel to have a husband to provide for her and to protect her and to give her a secure future — that was the basis of the Levirate marriage law.

Even though Ruth was a grown woman, Naomi respected her as a person and asked her permission to seek a husband for her. This action of Naomi's, coupled with Ruth's previous actions was highly indicative of the women's mutual love and respect for one another. Ruth asked for Naomi's permission to glean in the fields, and Naomi asked for Ruth's permission to find her a husband. Neither woman needed to ask the other for their permission, but they did.

****

What else does it say about the character of each woman when they would request the other's permission to do things that would affect the other person? (Ruth 2:1 and 3:1)

****

Naomi knew Boaz was their kinsman and she had investigated to see what he would be doing that very night — she had waited until the right time to set her plan in motion. Ruth was unaware of the provision of the kinsman-redeemer so Naomi had to explain it to her. Because Ruth was part of the family of Elimelech through her former marriage to his son, Mahlon, Naomi called Boaz "our" kinsman-redeemer.

Naomi had developed a ten step plan and she it gave to Ruth. We must remember that Ruth was to induce, not seduce, Boaz into being her kinsman redeemer. Ruth may have thought Naomi's plan sounded a little odd, yet because Ruth trusted Naomi, Ruth was willing to carry it out.

****

 The above statement as to Ruth's intentions is a very important declaration for us to keep in mind. What is the difference between these two words — induce and seduce?

****

Naomi's plan was set out for Ruth to follow:

➢ She told where Ruth was to go in the evening in order to find Boaz.

➢ She instructed Ruth to bathe — more than just cleansing, similar to a present-day bubble bath with aromatic oils added to the water.

➢ She told Ruth to put on her best smelling perfume. Boaz had been relatively close to Ruth while she had been working in his fields and now it was time that Boaz had a different scent of Ruth since

Ruth had a different plan in mind — not gleaning grain, but proposing marriage to an unsuspecting kinsman redeemer. Naomi wanted Boaz to understand that this was not Ruth the worker, but Ruth the woman.

➤ Naomi told Ruth to put on a festive dress since the end of the harvesting season was marked by times of celebration. Naomi wanted Boaz to not only smell a different Ruth, but to see a different Ruth.

➤ Naomi knew that Boaz was a man who liked to be with his workers and that he would be with them that evening to help celebrate the end of the harvest season. She instructed Ruth to go there later in the evening and wait until the timing of the next step in her plan.

➤ Ruth was instructed to wait until most of the festivities of the evening were over before going to the celebrations. Ruth was to make her presence very "low key."

➢ Ruth was to be sure she knew the place where Boaz was going to lay down for the evening. For security reasons, Boaz would sleep at the furthest position away from the crowd to be the first line of defense for his grain pile from any would be robbers. As Boaz would lay his shawl at this location, Ruth was to take notice of where it was located. There would be no lights, only the light of the stars and she need to know precisely where Boaz would be sleeping.

➢ After everyone had either gone home or had lain down around the grain pile, Ruth was to go to where Boaz was sleeping and uncover his feet.

➢ Ruth was to lie down at his feet and cover herself over with Boaz's shawl that he was using as a blanket for the cool night air. This was a symbol of a marriage proposal.

➢ Naomi knew that when Boaz woke up and found Ruth under his shawl at his feet that he would know that she was pro- posing marriage. Boaz had expressed some benevolence toward Ruth, but now it was time to take the relationship to the next level. Naomi knew that Boaz would understand and know what he needed to do next. She instructed Ruth to do whatever Boaz told her to do. It was only because Boaz was a godly man that Naomi could give this instruction to Ruth.

****

 What was the risk that Ruth and Naomi could have been taking had Boaz not been the man they thought he was?

****

It is very significant that she went at night and in the way she went. Since the first kinsman redeemer had not made a move to fulfill his responsibility, she did not want to force Boaz's move. She lay at his feet, a sign of great humility. She did it at night, away from other people, in order not to embarrass Boaz or put social pressure upon him to do what she wanted him to do; she let him know her intentions without forcing him to do anything that he did not want to do. Nor did she do it at the city gate in front of many people.

Boaz had taken the first step in the barley field, Ruth had reciprocated on the threshing floor, and Naomi told Ruth to wait for Boaz's response on what to do next. The plan was all laid out and ready to be put into action.

Ruth Proposed Marriage to Boaz (3:6-13)

It was the custom to winnow the grain of the harvest at night. It was cooler then and the evening winds picked up, which enabled the workers to be more efficient. The threshing floor was a round space in the middle of the field (25 to 40 feet in diameter) where the sheaves of grain were brought to be winnowed. The floor was a space built upon a rocky surface or a hard soil area. It was usually built upon an elevated area where there would be a constant evening breeze present to blow away the chaff. Winnowing the grain involved throwing the wheat up into the air so the wind would then blow away the chaff and the wheat, which was heavier, fell back to the ground. Then a sieve was used to separate dirt and other impurities that mixed in with the grain during the process of winnowing. This was a joyous time at the end of the harvest with a lot of celebration by the workers and the field owner alike.

In accordance with Naomi's plan, Ruth crept up and covered herself with Boaz's shawl. This was a marriage proposal; Ruth was saying to Boaz by this act, "I desire to become your wife." (See Ezekiel 16:8)

Around midnight, Boaz awoke startled at someone lying at his feet. He was startled mainly because he did not know what was going on, nor knowing who was at his feet. When Ruth acknowledged who she was, she asked Boaz to spread his covering over her. She had covered herself indicating her desire for marriage, now she asked him to cover her and waited for his response.

Boaz accepted Ruth's proposal and he knew what to do. Boaz gave an immediate and positive response to Ruth's proposal. He thought Ruth's kindness to Naomi in coming back with her was highly commendable, but he felt this was even greater. He stated that he would do everything she asked of him, i.e. marriage, and he once again praised her character over her physical beauty. He gave her a vow that he would do all within his power as soon as he could to secure their marriage.

****

 Since Boaz's response was so immediate and positive, do you think he had previously thought about this possibility?

****

Now things are starting to move a little faster. Boaz told Ruth to lie covered at his feet until early morning and then she needed to leave while it was yet very dark. Boaz was protective of Ruth's reputation and did not want her presence with him to be misunderstood. In the Mishnah, there is a provision (Yeb 2:8) that says if a Jewish man is even suspected of being immoral with a Gentile woman, he is disqualified from ever being a kinsman redeemer. This Boaz said as if in a prayer to the Lord God for his protection, as well as for Ruth's. ". . . Let it not be known that the woman came to the threshing floor." (Ruth 3:14)

As she went, Boaz gave Ruth six measures of barley to take with her. He knew that from this day forward, Ruth's gleaning days were over. This was over six times the amount she had gleaned earlier from the fields (2:17). Earlier, Boaz had made a comment about Ruth returning with Naomi, he again makes reference to Naomi's statement she had made when she had returned (1:21, "I came back empty"). Now, Boaz responds to that statement in saying to Ruth, "Do not go back empty" (Ruth 3:17). All the while this was going on between Ruth and Boaz, Naomi was home alone and probably had not slept a wink all night, waiting for Ruth's return.

****

 What do you think Naomi was doing while Ruth was at the harvest celebration carrying out the ten-step plan for proposing marriage to Boaz?

****

After hearing from Ruth about Boaz's positive response, Naomi knew the matter would be settled the same day. Perhaps Boaz had a reputation as a man of action in getting things done in a hurry. Both Boaz and Ruth must have had a great deal of difficulty in containing their exuberance over what they thought could very well be their future together.

Wrap Up

1. Like all godly endeavors, Ruth's actions had three necessary components:
   (1) a Biblical basis,
   (2) the right mix of faith and works, and
   (3) the timing of the Lord for its fulfillment.

2. The key to any relationship is the integrity of the people involved, whether it is in marriage, or any other type.

3. The manner in which Ruth proposed marriage to Boaz was a reflection of her character. She came in humility, with sensitivity, and was not demanding; she knew that to force him to do what she wanted him to do would produce short term results with long term damage to the relationship.

4. Waiting upon the Lord, or anyone else for that matter, is one of the hardest things to do. And yet it is often the most important part in seeing the Lord work His plan.

Scene #5

A Man on a Mission
Ruth 4:1-12

How would you like to ride in a car that was being driven by someone who, when faced with any situation, had to consult the driver's manual to see what to do? When he came to an intersection, he had to look up who had the right of way? A crash could have occurred before he found the answer. Or when he came to a stop sign, he had to look up what it really meant. I think that when it comes to riding with someone, I want a driver who already knows what the manual says and is able to drive according to it. Or, how would you like to go to the hospital to have surgery when the surgeon came in carrying text books on how to do the surgery he or she was going to perform on you? Or, what would you think if you saw the airline pilot enter the cockpit carrying a book, "Flying Airliners for Dummies"? Get the picture? There is a time for learning and there is a time to do what needs to be done. When it comes to the crucial issues of life, we need to know what the manual says before we take on the task.

This is what Boaz did. He knew the manual (the Holy Scriptures). He had studied the role of the kinsman redeemer and knew what needed to be done. He then waited until the appropriate time when he could apply the Scriptures accurately to his situation. The outcome was that a godly union was about to be formed that would one day bring forth a son who would become a part of the lineage of the Lord Jesus Christ. It all points back to the true saying, *God's work done God's way produces God's results.*

The Meeting at the Gate (4:1-6)

There was a seven step process required by the one who was to be the kinsman redeemer:

✝ Getting witnesses to confirm every transaction between all possible redeemers.

✝ Agreement on which man shall be the redeemer — Ruth 4:3-6.

✝ Taking off the shoe of the one who gives his right of redemption to another, as a witness that he gives up such rights — Ruth 4:7-8.

✝ Redemption of the inheritance itself — Ruth 4:9.

✝ Marriage between the redeemer and the wife of the dead one to raise up children to continue his name — Ruth 4:10.

✝ Confession of witnesses to the transaction — Ruth 4:11.

✝ Blessing of the married couple — Ruth 4:11-12.

Is It By Chance or By Divine Design?

This is an example of the practical out-working of verses such as: Romans 8:28 and Psalm 37:23.

And we know that God causes all things to work together for good to those who love God, to those who are called according to His purpose. (Romans 8:28)

When a man loves the Lord God and knows His calling upon his life, and follows it out of love for Him, then God causes everything that happens to that man to work out for his ultimate good and God's glory.

The steps of a man are established by the Lord, and He delights in his way. Psalm 37:23)

When a man follows in the way the Lord has designed for his life, then all that he does brings delight to the Lord God. And not only that, but there is joy in knowing I am following the Lord and doing what He has for my life.

****

Digging Deeper — Romans 8:28

Frequently believers read this verse and wonder why they are not experiencing more good things in their lives. They may feel that this verse tells us that if we love the Lord Jesus and are called to Him, then only good things are to happen to them. But that is not what the verse says, nor is it what it means.

Romans 8:28 reminds me of one of my favorite foods — chocolate cake. If we take each of the ingredients of chocolate cake and taste them individually, none of them taste good. However, put them all together and mix them up, then put them in a cake pan, then into the oven for the right time and WALLAH — a wonderfully tasting chocolate cake.

This verse is like a chocolate cake. Taken individually, the events of our lives may not taste very good at all, they may even taste awful — like the baking soda in a choco- late cake. But when the Lord Jesus takes all the ingredients of our life and mixes them together and then puts us occasionally into the fires of adversity, He produces in us His character and causes us to become more like His Son, Jesus Christ (Romans 8:29).

So when you think of Romans 8:28, think of chocolate cake. Not all the events of life are good individually, but they do work together for our good, and for His glory.

****

Boaz was a man who knew the Lord and tried his best to follow His ways. As a result, the Lord God was able to guide his life and bring all He had planned for him to pass.

The city gate served two main purposes: (1) it was the place where all the legal business of the city was transacted; both city officials and local residents went there to conduct their legal business. And (2) it was the place where people passed through to enter and leave the city. Boaz thought that his relative might pass through the gate, but since the man was also a field owner, it was not a sure thing. Like Boaz, when I am seeking the Lord's will and I wait upon Him, then He will bring the right people, at the right time, into my path.

Why didn't Ruth plead her case for herself? That was what the Levirate marriage law said she was to do (Deuteronomy 25:5-10). However, the law also forbids a Moabite from entering into an assembly of Israel (Deuteronomy 23:3). Boaz knew this and went to the gate of the city to act on Ruth's behalf.

What a picture this is of the Lord Jesus going to the Father to act upon our behalf. We could not approach the Father on our own because of our great sin, but only Jesus as our great kinsman redeemer could do it on our behalf, being a man and being the only one qualified to redeem us.

An important issue at the heart is the law of the kinsman redeemer was this — who owned the land? The land of Israel belonged to the Lord God (Leviticus 25:23). If for any reason an Israelite sold his land to another

Israelite, the sale was never final, nor was the title deed ever transferred. Either the man himself or one of his close relatives could redeem the land for him at any time and pay a redemption price prorated to the time the land was used (Leviticus 25:24-25). At the year of the Jubilee, every 50th year, all property that had been sold reverted back to its original owner or to his heirs (Leviticus 25:26-28). An Israelite did not own the land, God owned it, and thus the Israelites were stewards of God's land.

When Elimelech left Bethlehem, it was a certainty that he owned land and a home because he was an Ephrathite, a member of the upper level of society. Further, when Elimelech left Bethlehem, he was intending to stay away only a short while so he probably would not have sold his land or home. Now since Naomi stayed in Moab over ten years with no stated means of employment or source of income, she most likely sold some of the land in Bethlehem and had the funds sent to her at Moab.

Then when Naomi and Ruth returned to Bethlehem, the women had a home in which to live, but no land to sell for income with which to buy food. So Ruth resorted to gleaning. Now, Boaz wants to redeem the land for Naomi, knowing Ruth's rightful claim upon the land would complicate the transaction. For the first kinsman redeemer, Ruth would pose a major problem, but not for Boaz.

The issue is the same for us today. Because I acknowledge Jesus Christ as my Lord, He owns all that I am and all that I have and I am but a steward over it all. Sometimes we might be tempted to say, "What I own, I purchased with my own money that I myself earned." However we forget that the Lord has given us even the ability to earn money (Deuteronomy 8:18) and we do not have anything that has not come from Him (1 Corinthians 4:7). We must hold on loosely to all that He has given so that we will be able to say as Job said,

The Lord gave and the Lord has taken away. Blessed be the name of the Lord. (Job 1:21b)

****

 How would you describe the role of a "steward," and how does it differ from the role of an owner?

What does the Lord require of a steward? (1 Corinthians 4:2)

Do you consider yourself an owner or a steward of all that you have?

****

The Transaction had to be a Legal Transfer

The Mishnah was a collection of oral traditions of the rabbi's that later became the Talmud in written form. It was not the Law of God, but how the rabbi's interpreted the Law as applied to specific situations. The Mishnah required at least ten elders of the city to hear a case in order to make it a legal transaction. However, the Law only required two or three witnesses to make a transaction legal — Deuteronomy 17:6-7; 19:15. This requirement

was carried on into the New Testament proce-
dures as well — Matthew 18:16; 2 Corinthians
13:1; 1 Timothy 5:19; and Hebrews 10:28.

As the twelve men began discussing the
matter amongst themselves, a crowd soon gath-
ered around them. Notice in the following
chart the five requirements for a man to be
a kinsman redeemer, and how the Lord Jesus
became our kinsman redeemer.

The Five Requirements	*The Lord Jesus Christ*
He had to be a **_near_** relative.	Jesus Christ became a man in order that He redeem us from our sin — Galatians 4:4-5, Philippians 2:5-9, Romans 8:3, and Hebrews 2:14, 17
He had to be **_willing_** to redeem the land for his relative.	Jesus Christ willingly gave His life to redeem us — Mark 10:45, John 10:17-18, Galatians 1:4, Ephesians 5:2, Titus 2:13-14, and 1 John 3:16.

He had to be financially and legally *able* to redeem the land for his relative.	Because Jesus Christ is the only one who is sinless, He is the only one able to redeem us — 2 Corinthians 5:21, 1 Peter 2:22, and 1 John 3:5.
He had to be *free* himself before he could redeem another.	Jesus Christ was, and is, the only one free from sin so He could redeem us from our sin — Luke 23:41, 47, John 8:46, and Hebrews 4:15.
He must have the *price* of the redemption and be able to pay in legal tender that which was acceptable to the one who held the land.	Jesus Christ gave His life as the payment price paid in full for our redemption — John 3:16, Romans 5:8, 1 Corinthians 15:3 & 6:20, Hebrews 9:26, and 1 Peter 2:24 & 3:18,.

A Legal Glitch

The first kinsman redeemer hit a legal snag in his agreement to redeem the land for Naomi. Elimelech had previously owned the land and he had two sons, but all three of these men had died. The ownership of the land then reverted to Naomi, but she most likely would not produce a male heir to inherit the land from her. Ruth, being the wife of one of Elimelech's sons, could very possibly have a legal right to contest the land being sold to someone she did not like, because she had become a convert to Judaism, in espousing the God of Naomi (Ruth 1:16).

Although it was not the normal case, the redemption of the land in this case was directly tied to the Levirate marriage provision of the Law. When Boaz pointed this out to the man, he immediately backed off because a possible legal entanglement over Elimelech's land being passed on to his sons could jeopardize his own son's inheriting his own land one day.

One thing to keep in mind is that when we are passionate about doing what we believe to be the will of God for our lives, obstacles will always be a part of the process. But they are things to be overcome, not roadblocks to halt the process. As soon as the first man declined, Boaz immediately accepted. Boaz knew the Scriptures and how to correctly apply them to appropriate situations. Most likely he had thought through this scenario many times over and now it had come to pass.

****

Digging Deeper — Godly Wisdom

Godly wisdom is knowing what the Scriptures are that are appropriate to a given situation and how to correctly apply them.

****

The Power of the Shoe (4:7)

Did you know there is the power in the shoe? In the days of the Old Testament, feet and shoes had symbolic meaning; some common meanings were:

- Placing the foot or the shoe on something or upon someone showed possession

of, or power over something or someone
— Joshua 10:24 & Psalm 8:6; 60:8; 08:9.

- To set foot on land symbolized ownership of it — Deuteronomy 1:36; 11:24
and Joshua 1:3; 14:9.

- Removing shoes in another's presence symbolized submission to their
authority — Exodus 3:5 and Joshua 5:15
— or powerlessness and humiliation — 2
Samuel 15:30 & Isaiah 20:2-4 & Ezekiel
24:17, 23.

- From the beginning, God told Abraham
that where ever he walked that He would
give that land to him (Genesis 13:17).
When a man purchased a piece of land
he would walk around it to signify his
ownership. And when He removed his shoe
and gave it to another, it symbolized a
transfer of ownership of the land being
discussed.

When the first kinsman redeemer removed his
sandal and gave it to Boaz, he was signifying
his relinquishing of his right to buy back

the land for Naomi, and thus for marrying Ruth as well.

It's a Done Deal!

As soon as the unnamed man relinquished his right of redemption, Boaz immediately called upon the elders and all the people to acknowledge what they had just heard and seen. All that was formerly Elimelech's, Chilion's, and Mahlon's could now be redeemed by paying back the one(s) who had bought it from Naomi.

Whenever the land had been previously sold and to whomever it had been sold is not known. At the time of this transaction, Boaz had now suddenly redeemed it for Naomi. Further, at that very moment Boaz redeemed the land for Naomi he was legally married to Ruth.

****

Digging Deeper — The Jewish Wedding Ceremony

In the Jewish wedding process, there were, and still are, three steps to getting married. The process began with a legal commitment made between the parents, at which the couple was married even though they do not live together as husband and wife. The second step is a period of three to six months when each one prepared individually for living together as husband and wife. The end of this time period would be determined by the groom's father. The man would prepare a home in which he and his wife would live together. The wife would gather her things and both mentally and physically get herself ready to live with her husband in the home he had made. The third stage consummated the wedding when the groom went to get his bride and brought her back to his newly finished home. A wedding feast marked the completion of the wedding process and the man and woman lived together as husband and wife.

Doesn't this sound like what Jesus has done for us? We are His bride, the church. He came and paid the price for His bride and now He has gone back to heaven to prepare a place for us (John 14:3a). We are left here, legally bound to Jesus yet not living together with Him. When the time is right He will come and take us home to heaven (John 14: 3b) and then we will live in a mansion prepared for us. There will also be a wedding feast that is prepared for us that will mark the consummation of the wedding of the Lord Jesus Christ and His Bride — the Church (Revelation 19:7-10).

****

The Blessing of the People

The people standing around gave a three part blessing over the marriage of Boaz and Ruth. **First,** they prayed that God would give Ruth many children and that she would raise up a generation to be blessed and used like

Rachel and Leah had done through Jacob. The **second** blessing is somewhat difficult to translate into English, but it gives the idea that because of the children that Ruth would give to Boaz he would prosper because of them and become a famous man — all of this came to pass in that through their son Obed, Boaz and Ruth obtained a place in the genealogy of our Lord Jesus Christ. **Third,** the house of Perez had obtained a status of preeminence throughout Judah and the people blessed Ruth and Boaz with the same hope for their future generations.

It is good to have a group of people around you whose views and opinions are important to you. Not everyone's opinion carries equal value, but it is important to have a counsel of the wise to guide us through life's decisions. This is especially so with the selection of a marriage partner. These important people in our lives often have a more objective view of the two people about to enter into the marriage. They may have insights unclouded by "love," making their views more objective. Seeking the blessing of one's "important people" on their coming marriage will add a sense of great confidence to the marriage relationship. When they withhold their blessing it is time to stop and ask "why?".

What do you do when they express grave opinions about the person you are about to marry and they withhold their blessing? There are three things you must do.

- Take your time, don't be in any hurry. These people have opinions that you have held as being important in the past and their negative reaction is worthy of your investigation. Do they have these feelings based upon their observations, or does your potential marriage partner remind them of someone else?
- Seek the counsel of a pastor or spiritual advisor.
- When all is said and done, remember you can seek the counsel of others, but you alone must make the final decision.

This is a blissful ending to the life of Naomi who had earlier given five accusations against God (1:13, 20-21).

o   The hand of the Lord is against me (1:13).
o   The Almighty has dealt very bitterly with me (1:20).
o   I went out full, but the Lord has brought me back empty (1:21).
o   The Lord has witnessed against me (1:21).
o   The Almighty has afflicted me (1:21).

When Naomi made these statements, she had no idea of the great things that the Lord God was going to do for her.

There may be some times in the life of the Believer when they may also be tempted to make such accusations against God. Just as Naomi did, Jacob made such accusations when he said,

And their father Jacob said to them, "You have bereaved me of my children: Joseph is no more, and Simeon is no more, and you would take Benjamin; ***all***

these things are against me. " [Genesis 42:36, emphasis mine]

In both instances, neither Naomi nor Jacob were aware of the great things that God was orchestrating behind the scenes for their lives.

There may also be times when we are tempted to make such accusations against the Lord God, when things do not seem to be going the way we think they should. When those times come, there is a major guiding principle that should be our guide in thinking things through — Jeremiah 29:11.

"For I know the plans that I have for you," declares the Lord, "plans for welfare and not for calamity to give you a future and a hope." [Jeremiah 29:11]

Israel thought they knew what God was doing for them, but they were mistaken. It was as if God was saying "You think you know, but you really don't. Only I know the plans I have . . ." They did not understand that all that was happening to them was for their benefit which would result in giving them a bright future and a secure hope. The same holds true for us today.

Wrap Up

1. God uses people who have taken the time and energy to prepare themselves to be used of God by studying the Word of God and knowing how to accurately interpret and apply it to life situations. So the prayer of our hearts should not be, "Lord, use me!" Instead, it should be, "Lord make me useable!" For when we are useable, He will use us to the maximum.

2. Understanding the importance of timing in doing the work of the Lord and waiting until it is right is a major help in serving the Lord effectively. Consider the following paradigms:

   • The right thing at the wrong time will bring frustration.
   • The wrong thing at the right time will bring failure.

- The right thing at the right time will bring success.

3. The author of the book of Ruth took great pains not to embarrass the man who was first in line to be the kinsman redeemer, since it was not in God's plan for him to be the one to redeem the land and to marry Ruth.

4. Because Boaz and Ruth had acted out of their integrity and had followed the directions of the Scriptures, they received the blessing of the people of the city upon their lives and their marriage.

Scene #6

Make Lemonade When God Hands You Lemons
Ruth 4:13-17

For the true believer, there is never a hopeless situation. It was not hopeless when Abraham was called to sacrifice Isaac because at the very last minute, a ram appeared to become Isaac's substitute. It was not hopeless when Joseph's brothers threw him into the pit and then sold him into slavery. In the end God raised him up to be a national leader, second only to Pharaoh himself. It was not hopeless when Job lost all he had and his friends and wife turned against him. Then God gave him twice what he had in the beginning. It was not hopeless when Jesus arrived in Bethany at Mary and Martha's home because He had come to raise Lazarus from the dead. In all these instances, God raised up a new testimony of His faithfulness to His people. And He still does it today.

Life seemed pretty hopeless when Naomi and Ruth first came back to Bethlehem. Then God restored their hope and raised up a new testimony of Himself through them. Remember, never count the score at half time. *There is always hope . . . it isn't over, till it's over.*

Fast Forward through the Next Year (4:13)

When reading the Word of God, always keep in mind the time factor of the passage which you are reading. For instance, consider the time factor in the different passages of Ruth's story.

✞ Ruth 1:1-5 = ten years.
✞ Ruth 1:6-22 = one or two months.

✝ Ruth 2:1-23 = seven weeks.

✝ Ruth 3:1-18 = one night.

✝ Ruth 4:1-12 = one day.

✝ Ruth 4:13-17 = approximately one year.

✝ Ruth 4:18-22 = 900 years

Five Major Events

There were five major events in the year following Boaz's meeting at the gate.

- Boaz took Ruth. This was the engagement period where Boaz had prepared his house for his new bride and Ruth had to gather her things and prepare herself to be Boaz's wife. This time of preparation usually took three to six months.
- And she became his wife. Marriage is a life-long, growing process, not merely an event. The act of commitment is a vital part of the marriage process.

****

Digging Deeper —
The Commitment of Marriage

Some say they do not need a "piece of paper" to show their love for one another. There are two major flaws to this answer. First, it is more than just a "piece of paper" it is a commitment of intent. Would you sell a house without a "piece of paper?" Would you loan someone a large sum of money without a "piece of paper?" Would you buy a car without a "piece of paper?" Would you enter into any type of major agreement without a "piece of paper?" Marriage is an agreement much more important than possessions or finances.

Second, not having that "piece of paper" sends a confusing message to the partner. It says "I am committed to you, but not to the point of my being willing to make it into a written document." It says, "I will make a limited commitment to you but I will still leave myself an out so that I can walk away at any time I want with no consequences from doing so."

****

- And he went in to her. The physical union of marriage is to be entered into in purity (Hebrew 13:4). Because people are composed of a three part entity (1 Thessalonians 5:23), the physical oneness of marriage is to be preceded by a spiritual oneness and a soulish oneness.
- And the Lord enabled her to conceive. On one hand, children are a gift from God (Psalm 127:3) and on the other hand they are loaned to us (1 Corinthians 4:7) from Him to be raised for Him. There are always God's purposes in both enabling conception and in withholding conception.

****

In one verse (Ruth 4:13), in 29 words, God compressed one whole year of Boaz and Ruth's life activities. What is the underlying message that the Lord God is saying here by the apparent lack of information?

****

- And she gave birth to a son. There are twelve variables that go into every person who is born; gender is only one of those twelve.

  [Note: the other eleven variables are (1) time in history, (2) parents, (3) birth order, (4) ethnic heritage, (5) cultural background, (6) physical features, (7) brothers and/or sisters (or lack of them), (8) mental abilities, (9) the aging and death process, (10) our uniqueness — expressed in our DNA, our finger prints, our voice patterns, our retina construction, and our dental patterns, and (11) our spiritual gift given by the Holy Spirit.]

In the formation of life, God never makes mistakes. Each person has God's perfect design for his or her life (Exodus 4:11; Jeremiah 1:5; Psalm 139:13).

* *

 Given the twelve birthing factors, what are the probabilities of two people being "constructed" alike? To further complicate this probability, factor in the seven motivational gifts of Romans 12:3-8 (prophecy, serving, teaching, exhorting, giving, leading, and mercy), one of which every Christian has been given and the probability of two people being constructed alike is 1:(an astronomical figure too high to calculate).

How does 2 Corinthians 10:12 add anything to this thought?

* *

Naomi Received a Blessing of Hope for the Future (4:14-15)

When Naomi had first returned from Moab to Bethlehem, she had no hope. She came back empty. She came back defeated. She came back angry at God for the way He had treated her. Things had changed for Naomi and Ruth. Now the women of Bethlehem gave her a blessing of renewed hope in view of Boaz and Ruth.

- The Lord did not leave her without a redeemer.
- The Lord will restore your life out of your hopeless past.
- The Lord gave her a sustainer in her old age.

The Big Difference a Baby can Make in a Family (4:16-17)

In a very real sense, the child belongs to Naomi. Boaz was the kinsman redeemer for Naomi since her husband, Elimelech, had died without a son to carry on his inheritance.

Even the women of Bethlehem said a son had been born to Naomi (4:17). In an unusual move, the woman of Bethlehem named the child. There are only two other instances in the Biblical record where someone other than the parents named their child — John the Baptist (Luke 1:13) and Jesus (Matthew 1:21). This suggests that the birth of the child was an important event that concerned the whole town of Bethlehem.

The name given to the child, Obed, means "servant." Obed would serve Naomi in assuring her that Elimelech's inheritance of the land would not be lost to future generations. Obed would also serve the purposes of the Lord in raising up a son, Jesse, and on through David until we come to the birth of our Savior, Jesus Christ.

****

 Why do you think the women were allowed to name the child "Obed?"

****

The goal is not just to raise children, but to raise up a godly generation. God was, and is today, moving through history to bring all things to a climatic conclusion of the end time events (Hebrews 1:3).

*And He is the radiance of His glory and the exact representation of His nature, and **upholds** all things by the word of His power. (Hebrews 1:3)*

The word translated here "upholds" means "to carry something along to its expected end; to carry something to where it belongs." The Lord God is carrying all of human history towards the end times that He has before preordained to be. Every generation unfolds an important part of that plan of God for the ages, bringing us closer and closer to that glorious day when time shall be no more.

Ruth was unaware of God's greater purpose for her life. She did not see all of the things that the Lord God would do through her life while she was alive. Serving the Lord and living for Him means we make life investments that will continue to pay eternal dividends long after we have left this earth. These eternal dividends will far outweigh any personal cost or sacrifice we are called upon to make.

****

Digging Deeper — Sacrifice

Sometimes the Lord Jesus calls us to do a ministry or to perform a particular service. Often these tasks will include a personal cost or a sacrifice. It is good to count the cost of any endeavor, but when we focus upon the personal cost or sacrifice then we tend to become discouraged and want to give up. Rather than focus upon the cost, it is better to concentrate upon the effect of what the ministry or service will produce. It is only when we focus upon the eternal results that the personal cost diminishes.

In speaking about the Lord Jesus in Hebrews 12:2, the Bible records, ". . . who before the joy set before Him endured the cross . . ." Scripture records a time in the life of the Lord Jesus when He did focus His mind upon the cross (Luke 22:41-44), but that time came and it passed. What remained was the "joy that was set before Him." That is, He focused upon the multitudes of lives that would be redeemed by His work upon the Cross. He thought about the change the world would experience because of Believers who would be "salt and light" (Matthew 5:13-16) to an unbelieving world. He thought about the ultimate defeat of Satan. All of this brought Him unspeakable joy and that became the focus of His mind at the Cross. Then the time for the Cross came, it was something merely to "endure" rather than to govern His thoughts.

A sacrifice is only a sacrifice when we focus upon the sacrifice. But when we focus upon the eternal significance or the work, the sacrifice becomes something much smaller to be endured in order to accomplish the eternal results. Where is your focus?

****

Coming Around Full Circle

When we consider all things, the story in the book of Ruth brings us right back to where we began — only much better. Compare the opening verses of Ruth 1:1-5 with the closing verses of Ruth 4:13-17 in the following chart:

Ruth 1:1-5		*Ruth 4:13-17*
A famine in Bethlehem	*The Situation*	A wedding in Bethlehem
Arriving in Moab	*Family Status*	Established back in Bethlehem
Marriage, then deaths	*Family Events*	Marriage, then a birth
Barrenness	*Children*	Birth of a son
No hope	*Possibility of Help*	A bright future

Widow of Naomi's son	*Status of Ruth*	Better than seven sons
Emptiness and grief because of death of her husband and two sons	*Naomi's Emotions*	Joyfulness and hope over Boaz and Ruth's marriage and Obed's birth
Half time; half time scores never count, it only serves to show where adjustments need to be made	*Game Time*	Final score; only the final score really matters

In looking at the chart, we see the left column represents life in the hands of people who live in opposition to God's Word. The right column represents all the blessings that God can give to those whose lives are lived in obedience to Him and His Word.

Wrap Up

1. The Lord God has also raised up a Redeemer for us in the Lord Jesus Christ. He takes lives that have been broken, abused, cast off, and wrecked and He redeems us with new life in Him.

2. In our new life in the Lord Jesus He restores our life from the hopeless past to give us meaning and purpose in life. Often He will take our past experiences and attach new meanings to them as a testimony of praise for Himself through us.

3. He also becomes our sustainer and provider to give us all we need in Him to live for Him and serve Him. We can trust in Him for all we need.

4. When we live in obedience to Him, He will bless us and refine us to make us more like Him.

5. In the life of the Christian, there is never a hopeless situation. It may just be

half time or some other point in the game, but there is always hope, because the Lord Jesus Christ is in control.

Epilogue

Life Goes On, Generation after Generation
Ruth 4:18-22

This last passage of Ruth reminds me of when we put up our Christmas tree. The tree itself is a thing of beauty with its bubble lights, twinkling lights, glass balls, and all the glittering decorations. Yet no Christmas tree is complete until the star is put on top and it is lit.

The book of Ruth is like the tree, and these last five verses are the star that makes the book complete — a sight of great beauty. We often bypass genealogies concluding they are obsolete or meaningless. However 2 Timothy

3:16 tells us that "all Scripture is given by inspiration of God and is profitable . . ."

The last five verses of Ruth are directly connected to the following two verses:

(1) Proverbs 25:2, *It is the glory of God to conceal a matter, but the glory of kings is to search out a matter*

(2) Deuteronomy 17:18-20, *Now it shall come about when he sits on the throne of his kingdom, he shall write for himself a copy of this law on a scroll in the presence of the Levitical priests. It shall be with him and he shall read it all the days of his life, that he may learn to fear the Lord his God, by carefully observing all the words of this law and these statutes, that his heart may not be lifted up above his countrymen and that he may not turn aside from the commandment, to the right or the left, so that he and his sons may continue long in his kingdom in the midst of Israel.*

Only the King had a personal copy of the Scriptures, but today we all have our personal copy of the Word of God, so Proverbs 25:2 also applies to us. These five verses are a gold mine for those willing to dig in and search out the matter.

There are 16 Generational Lists Recorded in the Word of God.

When we come to generational lists in the Bible, we tend to rush right over them or else we skip them altogether. However, generational lists seem to be an important thing for the Lord God since He put fourteen such lists in the Old Testament and two in the New Testament.

- o The generations of the heavens and the earth (Genesis 2:4).
- o The generations of Adam (Genesis 5:1-32).
- o The generations of Noah (Genesis 6:9-10).
- o The generations of the sons of Noah (Genesis 10:1-32).

o The generations of Shem (Genesis 11:10-11).

o The generations of Terah (Genesis 11:27).

o The generations of Ishmael (Genesis 25:12-18).

o The generations of Isaac (Genesis 25:19-26).

o The generations of Esau (Genesis 36:1-8).

o The generations of the sons of Esau (Genesis 36:9-43).

o The generations of Jacob (Genesis 37:2)

o The generations of Moses and Aaron (Numbers 3:1)

o The generations of Pharaz (Ruth 4:18).

o The generations of Adam to David (1 Chronicles 1-9).

****

 What benefits do you see for the genealogies?

****

There is unique value in the generational list of Ruth 4:18. Ruth's list gave the earliest record of the two genealogies of David, giving him Scriptural authority to ascend to his throne. Ruth's list was written during the time of the Judges — a period of around 300 years beginning in 1370. Whereas the 1 Chronicles 1-9 record was written much later (c.450 - 425 B.C.), towards the end or shortly after the period of Judah's Babylonian Captivity. Ruth's list alone validates the line of David from the tribe of Judah prior to his reign.

There are also two lists in the New Testament.

o The generation of Abraham through David to Solomon to Joseph — the royal line (Matthew 1:1-18).

o The generation of Adam through David to Nathan to Mary, the mother of Jesus — the legal line (Luke 3:23-38).

****

Digging Deeper — The Genealogies of Jesus in Matthew and Luke

Why do the genealogies of Matthew and Luke vary so much? Why does one go from David through Solomon and the other go from David through one of his other sons, Nathan?

For the answer to these questions we need to look at Jeremiah 22:30 and 36:1-32. In Jeremiah 22:30, Jeremiah proclaims God's judgment upon Coniah:

Thus says the Lord, "Write this man down childless, a man who will not prosper in his days; for no man of his descendants will prosper sitting on the throne of David or ruling again in Judah.

Because of his actions, King Coniah of Judah was condemned by God in that not one of his offspring, which would one day include Jesus, would ever prosper on the throne of

David. This would affect the Lord Jesus Christ as He will one day, after His Second Coming, rule the world for 1,000 years from the throne of David (Isaiah 9:7). This is what we call the Millennial Reign of the Lord Jesus Christ (Revelation 20:1-6).

To further this line of God's judgment upon the kings of Judah, Jeremiah 36 tells of another story regarding the Kings of Judah. One time God gave a message to Jeremiah and Jeremiah had Baruch write it on a scroll and read it to the people in the area of the Temple. There one of the King's servants heard Baruch read God's message to the people and the servant told King Jehoiakim what he had heard. King Jehoiakim had the scroll brought to him and read in his presence. Part way through the reading, the King seized the scroll and cut it with a scribe's knife and threw it in the fire beside him. Later, Jeremiah had Baruch write the message down once again and the Lord God gave another judgment on King Jehoiakim and the royal descendants to come, which would include the Lord Jesus Christ.

Therefore thus says the Lord concerning Jehoiakim king of Judah, "He shall have no one to sit on the throne of David, and his dead body shall be cast out to the heat of the day and the frost of the night. I will also punish him and his descendants and his servants for their iniquity, and I will bring on them and the inhabitants of Jerusalem and the men of Judah all the calamity that I have declared to them — but they did not listen." (Jeremiah 36:30-31)

When we come to the Gospels of Matthew and of Luke, we see two different genealogies of Jesus. Matthew gives the royal lineage of David to Joseph; Luke gives us the legal lineage of David to Mary. Further examination of the two lineage records reveals that Matthew's genealogy comes from David through his son Solomon and on down to Joseph. However, Coniah and Jehoiakim are in the royal lineage from David through Solomon down to Joseph. If Jesus had been born of Joseph, He would be within the royal lineage for the throne of David, but He would also be under the curse of God from the two kings within His lineage. Because the royal lineage had been disqualified as the lineage through which the Messiah would one day come to rule the world from the throne of David, a second lineage took its place — another lineage from Joseph back through King David, through his next in line son, Nathan. The difficulty of these two genealogies is that Joseph is called the son of Jacob in Matthew's genealogy and at the same time he is called the son of Eli in Luke's genealogy. The answer is in the fact that in Jewish records of Genealogies, women do not normally appear. So when Joseph married Mary, he became known as Eli's son by marriage. So Matthew presents the royal lineage of David to Joseph and Luke presents the legal lineage of David to Mary. Therefore, it was necessary that Jesus be virgin born of Mary that He might be the legal heir to the throne of David, but still not fall under the judgments of the descendants of Joseph.

****

Who Are These People Anyway?

Looking through the cast of players that are listed in Ruth 4:18-22, we find that some of them are known a little, some are known a lot, and some are unknown.

First there was **Perez** — Judah had three sons, Er, Onan, and a much younger son named Shelah. (see Genesis 38) Er married Tamar, but Er was so wicked that the Lord God killed him. Following the custom of the levirate marriage that was designed to carry on the name of the deceased through a son, Judah told Onan, his second son, to marry Tamar and raise up a son for his dead brother. But Onan refused to raise up a son and the Lord God killed him also. Then Judah told Tamar to stay in his home and wait until Shelah was old enough and the third son would marry Tamar and raise up an heir. But when the time came and Shelah was old enough for marriage, Judah did not do what he said he would do. Then Tamar came up with a scheme to deceive Judah through an illicit affair with her and she conceived bearing twin sons (Perez and

Zerah). Then when it came time for Tamar to give birth to her twins, one extended his arm and a midwife tied a scarlet thread around its arm. Soon afterwards the arm with the thread was withdrawn and Perez was born. Afterwards, Zerah, the one with the thread around his arm was born. Perez and his family dominated the whole tribe of Judah and especially that of the city of Bethlehem.

It is extremely interesting to note that this genealogy begins with the name of a person who was the result of a failed attempt to implement the levirate marriage provision and in the middle is Obed, a person who was the result of a perfect example of how the levirate marriage provision was to function.

Perez and Obed are two examples of how the levirate marriage provision was to work. Perez is a failed example and Obed is a perfect example. With Perez, Tamar took matters into her own hands but with Ruth, she took things as far as she could and left the final work up to the authorities which God had placed over her. With Perez, the authorities over Tamar failed in carrying out their responsibilities, while with Ruth, the authorities over her faithfully carried out their responsibilities before the Lord.

Things always work out better when we do our part and wait patiently for the Lord to bring about the rest.

Second was **Hezron** — Little is known of Hezron, other than he was born in Caanan as the third son of Reuben (Exodus 6:14) and entered into Egypt with the rest of Israel (Genesis 46:12). A town at the southern border of Judah was named after him (Joshua 15:3).

Third is **Ram** — Not much is known of Ram; he was the second son of Hezron (1 Chronicles 2:9).

Fourth is **Amminadab** — The father-in-law of Aaron, the first High Priest of Israel, and the father of Nahshon, a leader of Israel in their journey to the Promised Land.

Fifth is **Nahshon** — He was the one who led the tribe of Judah as they camped and traveled throughout the wilderness journey (Numbers 2:3). Since Judah led the other eleven tribes when the nation moved at the direction of the Lord, Nahshon's leadership was a very important position (Numbers 10:14).

Sixth was **Salmon** — The father of Boaz by his wife, Rahab (Matthew 1:5).

Seventh in the list was **Boaz** — The kinsman redeemer for Elimelech and husband of Ruth. He was a man who became famous in Bethlehem (Ruth 4:11) as a model of godliness and graciousness. His name was engraved on one of the two pillars of the Temple (1 Kings 7:21 & 2 Chronicles 3:17) as a reminder of his godly character to all who entered the Temple.

Eighth in line was **Obed** — The son of Ruth, a Moabites and of Boaz.

Next was **Jesse** — The son of Obed and a well known farmer in Judah.

Last was **David** — The first king of Israel in fulfillment of the promise of Genesis 49:10. As King, David brought peace and prosperity to Israel. He became known as a man after God's own heart (Acts 13:22) and Israel's most beloved King.

What Is the Big Deal?

The Holy Spirit is laying the ground work, through the author of the book of Ruth, for the presentation of the credentials of David to be Israel's first king of the promise. The Holy Spirit is also precluding any objections to David being Israel's king because of him being the great grandchild of a gentile, Ruth the Moabitess. Without this lineage of David in the book of Ruth there could have been two main objections to David being King. Some could have objected on the basis that two descendents of his were Canaanites — Perez, the son of Tamar and Boaz, the son of Rahab.

****

 At what point did God desire Gentiles to enter into His kingdom? At the giving of what we call the "Great Commission?" What about Jonah being sent to Nineveh (Jonah 1:2)? Consider also these passages: Isaiah 49:6 (I will make you a

light for the Gentiles) & 56:7 (My house will be called a house of prayer for all nations).
****

There is a missing key to this passage — Genesis 49:10:

The scepter shall not depart from Judah, nor the ruler's staff from between his feet, until Shiloh comes, and to him shall be the obedience of the peoples.

It was prophesied that the ruler of Israel would always come from the descendants of Judah. This lineage of kings was to continue until Jesus Christ was to come and rule the nations.

This is super compressed history. The first five players in the passage represent the lineage from the giving of the promise until the wilderness journey of Israel — approximately 460 years. The second five players in the passage represent the lineage from the entrance into the Promised Land until the first of the Judean kings of Israel — approximately 440 years. These last five verses of Ruth connect the promise of God to the beginning of the fulfillment.

****

 When God's Word compresses history, does that mean that the people and events of the intermittent time had little value? What about the 2,000 years of Genesis 1 to 11 where only three stories are drawn out?

****

But Hold onto Your Socks

That is not all this passage holds in its meaning. I think there are two powerful messages contained in this genealogy. **The first message** is that God is always faithful to His Word. From the giving of the promise until it began to be realized was approximately 900 years. Consider these passages of Scripture that tell us what is demonstrated in this genealogy:

208

The Lord is not slow about His promise, as some count slowness, but is patient toward you . . . (2 Peter 3:9a)

God is not a man, that He should lie, nor a son of man, that He should repent; has He said, and will He not do it? Or has He spoken, and will He not make it good? (Numbers 23:19)

Now behold, today I am going the way of all the earth, and you know in all your hearts and in all your souls that not one word of all the good words which the Lord your God spoke concerning you has failed; all have been fulfilled for you, not one of them has failed. (Joshua 23:14)

Blessed be the Lord, who has given rest to His people Israel, according to all that He promised; not one word has failed of all His good promise, which He promised through Moses His servant. (1 Kings 8:56)

The second message this last passage of Ruth tells us is that history is really His story and every generation adds their part. God uses little known people to help unfold His plan. The process of history is not haphazard; there is a purpose in it all, and the purposes are the purposes of God.

****

 If God is always true to His Word, what does that mean to you personally?

****

A third message this passage holds for us is that even in the midst of turbulent times, like that of the Judges, God is still working. We are called to be transformed by the Word of God (Romans 12:1) and not to be conformed to the values of this world. God has always used people mightily who want their life to count for all eternity, who want the impact of their life to out-live them — people like Joseph, Daniel, Esther, Ruth, Boaz, etc.

A fourth message of this last passage is that even through the struggles of daily life, like with Naomi and Ruth, God is at work. God is as much in the struggles of life as He is in the good times. It is often in the times of struggle that we emerge in a newness of life, like the metamorphous of a caterpillar into a butterfly.

The final message of this passage is there is a continual plan of God that He is working to unfold. It began with Genesis 12:3 with the seven promises from the Lord God to His servant Abram. Four of these promises were for Abram personally (1, 2, 3, & 4). Three of these promises were for Abram's descendants — the nation of Israel (5 & 6). One of the promises is for the whole world (7).

1) I will make of you a great nation . . . .
2) I will bless you . . . . .
3) I will make your name great . . . .
4) You shall be a blessing . . . .
5) I will bless those who bless you . . . .

6) The one who curses you, I will curse . . . .

7) In you all the families of the earth will be blessed.

These seven promises are the beginning of the work of the Lord God which unfolds little by little in each generation until one day it will conclude with the four passages that are descriptive of the end of all history. These four passages will be completely fulfilled after the final judgment (Revelation 20:11) and we enter into eternity (Revelation 21 & 22).

- **Numbers 14:21** = *but indeed, as I live, all the earth will be filled with the glory of the LORD.*

- **Psalms 72:19**= *And blessed be His glorious name forever; and may the whole earth be filled with His glory.*

- **Isaiah 11:9** = *They will not hurt or destroy in all My holy mountain, for the earth will be full of the knowledge of the LORD AS the waters cover the sea.*

- **Habakkuk 2:14** = *For the earth will be filled with the knowledge of the glory of the LORD, as the waters cover the sea.*

God's redemptive plan for man continued unfolding with these seven promises to Abram. Its fulfillment will be concluded in eternity when His people dwell in perfect communion with Him.

God's redemptive plan is one of the themes in the book of Ruth. God is at work throughout history. Although Naomi, Ruth, and Boaz were not perfect, God was able to use them in the unfolding of His plan as they submitted their lives to Him. One day Ruth and Boaz's son, Obed, would take his place in the lineage of the Lord Jesus Christ.

Wrap Up

1. God is always working. He is not finished — with this world, or with you and me. As Philippians 2:13 states, *. . . for it is God who is at work in you, both to will and to work for His good pleasure.* Further, Ephesians 2:10 records, *For we are His workmanship* (a work in progress), *created in Christ Jesus for good works, which God prepared beforehand so that we would walk in them.* Where do you see the Lord at work in your life? What specific things has the Lord prepared for you to do? What distractions or obstacles have you encountered that hinder your effectiveness in doing these good works?

2. Naomi, Ruth, and Boaz left behind a legacy that lives on today. Have you considered what legacy you are leaving?

3. You may consider your life and obedience to Christ as ordinary and mundane, or

even insignificant. Yet each act of obedience contributes a vital part to God's overall plan. As each of the Old Testament believers and their stories led to the first coming of the Lord Jesus, our lives and our stories are leading up to His Second Coming. Where is it most difficult for you to continuously walk in obedience to the Lord?

4. When God gives a promise to us, we can hang on to it and rest assured that what He has said will become a reality one day. What promises has God given to you?

5. As Amos 3:7 states, *Surely the Sovereign LORD does nothing without revealing His plan to His servants the prophets.* God is in control and His plan is unfolding. How is the Lord using you to fulfill part of His redemptive plan?

CHALLENGE: If you are not able to easily identify your part in God's redemptive plan, I challenge you to fast and pray and ask the Lord what specific things He has for you to do. Then once you know what He has for you

to do, be diligent in doing them with love and devotion to Him.

One Final Project

List the life principles you have learned from your study in the book of Ruth. Here are two examples to get you started:

Life Principle #1 = I cannot escape God's discipline in my life.

Life Principle #2 = Godly character is developed by making right decisions, one after another, and not by conforming to the culture in which I live.

CPSIA information can be obtained at www.ICGtesting.com
Printed in the USA
LVOW13s2304130214

373443LV00002B/2/P

9 781626 976658